I FOUND SOMEONE
TO PLAY WITH

I FOUND SOMEONE
TO PLAY WITH

A BIOGRAPHY:
Larry LeGrande,
The Last Member of the Satchel Paige All-Stars

M. M. ANGELO

J. J. ANGELO

Cover design by Gian Philipp Rufin
Interior design by Mary Jean Archival
Technical Author J.J. Angelo
Author's Photo by Nancy Karmadi, MFA
Cary, NC 27519 USA

Published in the United States of America

ISBN: 978-0-578-19002-0
1. Biography & Autobiography / African American & Black
2. Biography & Autobiography / Sports
16.10.12

★ ★ ★

Acknowledgments

I would like to acknowledge and thank my husband Jim Angelo, Jr. who not only introduced me to Larry LeGrande, but was the inspiration and technical editing advisement in the writing of this historical window to baseball and the Negro League players.

I'm also grateful for my parents' life lessons and direction that has given me great inspiration, strength of heart and passion to forge new opportunities. My mother, Ann (Thibodeau) Letalien, of eighty-seven years, who to this day, as a steadfast New Englander in 2014 loves the game of baseball, in particular her beloved Boston Red Sox. My father, (Joseph Camille Thibodeau), who played baseball in Nova Scotia, Canada and later befriended Dom DiMaggio; remained an enthusiastic baseball fan until his passing in 1982.

Contents

* * *

Preface

My husband, Jim, played amateur baseball/softball in Ohio for thirty years. For seven years, he played and coached in the Roy Hobbs League as a pitcher and every other position on the field at least once, but mainly an outfielder just like Larry LeGrande. Incidentally, they share the same birthday, made their respective league's All-Star teams in their second year and came in second in the sprint race during tryouts. Being an undying fan of baseball, its history as well as the Negro Leagues, he soon discovered Larry LeGrande as he sat at his vendor table at the North Carolina State Fairgrounds with his historical memorabilia offerings from the American Negro Leagues of decades past. As Jim summoned me to the table and proceeded with the introduction, I soon found a strong desire to listen and learn of the Negro Leagues and Larry's life, challenges and perseverance as well as develop a newfound respect for these players. Thus, entered into a series of interviews with Larry.

This noble group of baseball players was relentlessly violated by the cold touch of unjust suspicion and prejudice. But this was a way of life—taking these dark challenges in stride, entombing the pain and staying focused on their goals. There was a deep determination and perseverance to stay positive and happy in trying to enjoy life. The game would exceed their expectations as they would rise to a celebrity status with money, vices, pride, and recognition only to fall as the Negro Leagues would dissipate as top talents was plucked from their teams into the Major Leagues. They were proud of their game—the way they played it and in turn proud of the recognition they attained.

I discovered a spirit that had been through trials and tribulations from an era that enforced laws under racial segregation preventing African-Americans from doing what most of the white people did.

This is written from a series of interviews with Larry LeGrande including an interview with his older sister. Although I've written on his behalf in first person from his interviews, I've added solely descriptive and additional explanations along with research for clarification purposes.

First, we need to examine what was happening with our culture and laws before and during the formation of the Negro Leagues. These laws were referred to as "Jim Crow" whereby they regulated things such as separate use of water fountains and separate seating sections in restaurants and public transportation and even separate hotels for blacks. (Jim Crow was a reference to a character in antebellum minstrel entertainment that was a racist stage depiction of poor and uneducated blacks).

These laws varied among communities and states, so it was difficult for the poor or uneducated black people to know the rules and laws if and when they crossed state lines because they never knew what to expect, many lived in fear for their lives. Some of these laws were passed immediately after the civil war called the "Black Codes". Although, the blacks were not always the targets of violence and oppression, many whites were as well when they attempted to support or show non-racial behaviors towards the blacks. The three main individuals who worked tirelessly to make modifications to lift the violence and oppression of the black racial challenges in this period were Rutherford B. Hayes, Ulysses S. Grant and Booker T. Washington. However, in the end, the Reconstruction period gave the black soldiers, individuals and businessmen the right to vote in the country.

Because blacks were not being accepted into the Major and Minor Baseball Leagues, they formed their own teams and created professional teams by the late 1800's. After the Civil War black baseball emerged in the Mid-Atlantic and Eastern states. The majority of the players were former military and key officers. The railroad industry was one of the largest and fastest growing employers, especially in the south.

Although cotton and tobacco within the agriculture industry was already established, it increased with the advent of industrialization, the end of World War II and service personnel returning from home to search for jobs. Some emerged from the railroad industry to play along with these strong military baseball greats.

Prior to the American Negro Leagues formation, they were known as the National Colored Baseball League. Some of the players were Cuban at the time as our country was on good terms with Cuba which in turn slowly increased the acceptance of Hispanics with the white players and patrons of the sport figures. However, many were hardened in their convictions and resolves over the prejudices and hatred of the times.

Kansas City, Missouri was the place where the Negro National League and its governing body the National Association of Colored Professional Baseball Clubs had first begun. The league was composed of eight teams, two of which were the Detroit Stars and the Kansas City Monarchs where Larry LeGrande eventually was called into action.

It was fifteen years before the Japanese attack on Pearl Harbor, Satchel Paige made his first appearance as a Chattanooga Black Lookout in 1926. In 1948 he had arrived in the Major Leagues with the Cleveland Indians amid tremendous controversy. Further, at an unofficial age of forty-two he was the oldest rookie in baseball as well as the first black pitcher. The Negro Leagues began to play with an assumption of future hostile intent. But they had an inner strength of spirit that their assurance of good nature would forestall hostility and the direful calamities of the time. That year, the Indians went on to win the World Series against the Boston Braves. Satchel was world champion in his first year in the big leagues!

My father, who had played semi-pro baseball in Nova Scotia, and all over the Maritime Provinces in Canada, had often talked of when the Negro League Baseball Players came into town, the Canadians would rush to play with them. The Canadians found that they were very good at their game, bound and determined to compete well and fair.

Many of the Canadian players were also military veterans, my father a veteran of the Royal Canadian Air Force enjoyed the competition. He had an extremely strong arm, with a blazing fast-ball and loved to mix things up with his respectable knuckle-ball pitch that would consistently baffle batters each and every trip to the mound. My mother told me that in his early days before they could afford a baseball glove, they'd use steak and tie it around their hand to catch the baseball. All the while, there was segregation and racial tension in the United States, the Canadian ball players didn't share the same perspectives and demonstrated a very different covenant when Negro ballplayers toured Canada.

As I shared my father's story with Larry, he smiled and said, "We never had any issues or racial problems in Canada." They enjoyed playing with the Canadians and looked forward to their trips with excitement and without fear. As Larry recalled one day in Canada, "We were going into a restaurant, and I returned to the bus to get a jacket—it was cold up there. The women would smile and say, 'Look at the darkies in there. We've never seen dark people before.' They stared and said, 'My! Aren't they dark!?' But these were good laughs when we got back on the bus."

A quote from Aristotle sums up the differences between anger and hatred:

> "Anger is always concerned with individuals... whereas hatred is directed also against classes: we all hate any thief and any informer. Moreover, anger can be cured by time; but hatred cannot. The one aims at giving pain to its object, the other at doing him harm; the angry man wants his victim to feel; the hater does not mind whether they feel or not."
>
> —Aristotle

It would seem that anger is a fleeting emotion that we've all experienced at one time or another. Anger is passion, and as one would have it, the worst of the seven deadly sins, leading one to temper and violence. Hatred on the other hand envelops malice, prejudice, animosity and venomous contempt. Has our American traditions and culture changed? With all the education available to us in this country have we learned? Why was it that the Canadians did not share these attitudes and behaviors when Americans did and in some cases still do to this day? Within this great country of ours there are answers to these questions, but they're buried deep inside ourselves in the spheres of our moral compass where the needle points to right or wrong, good or evil and love or hate. We all have choices—our choices are made from free will and the freedom that has been given to us as power, privilege and our right from our forefathers.

Sports segregation in the early 19th century was an immense issue with the players, teams and those who led them. In basketball for instance, the Harlem Globetrotters greatly influenced American acceptance of African-American players. In 1947, Jackie Robinson joined the Brooklyn Dodgers and not only broke the color barrier, but had a break-through season. Persistence of segregation and racial tension remained elevated through the 1960's when Larry LeGrande played for America's Negro Leagues.

My Inherent Talent
and Childhood

Life was not easy for Mom and Dad, however, in the early 19th century, for Negroes it was about survival. Making an honest life for yourself and your children as well as escaping the brutal life of American slavery and the slave trade. The threatening and oppressive Ku Klux Klan was growing larger, stronger, advocating death to black people who got in their way as well as recruiting some of the white civilians and community leaders in their legacy of evil, torture and murderous atrocities.

World War I lasted from 1914 to 1918. In the midst of this war, my father was drafted into the infantry, headed to France when the Armistice was declared and the ship was turned around. I guess it just wasn't his time. He later received an honorable discharge and went to work for the Norfolk Western railroad painting boxcars and working on the boilers afterwards for 0.38 cents an hour.

In 1929, the Great Depression devastated the United States. Hard times came to most people throughout the country, especially rural blacks. If jobs were to be found, the whites would attain the jobs. Cotton prices plunged from about eighteen to six cents a pound. Several million black farmers earned nothing or went into debt—people had no money to buy anything, much less food. Hundreds of thousands of agricultural workers or sharecroppers left for the cities, leaving behind abandoned fields and/or their homes. "Negro jobs"—jobs traditionally held by blacks, cotton and tobacco factory jobs, busboys, elevator operators, trash men, porters, maids, and cooks—were sought by desperate, unemployed whites. Moreover, in the Deep South, where blacks traditionally held menial jobs on trains, there was some safety, not only in numbers but also in the cities where segregation was flamboyant.

When the depression ended, my father came across a five-acre farm in Pinkard Court, close to Southern Hills near U.S. 220 in Mount Gilead near Roanoke Virginia in 1921. When he first laid eyes on the property and the small home, he stood there for the longest time surveying the land and the beautiful rich soil that would supply the sustenance for my family. Everywhere he turned, he was surrounded by the majesty of the mountains that consumed his soul. He also envisioned this farm as additional income for his family. Dad thought to himself this is ***THE PLACE*** where I'll raise my family. He set out to get it. Although my father was half white with lighter skin than most blacks, he didn't want to take any chances on missing out on this property with the white bankers. He had a Syrian friend called Mike George who lived nearby, making a living as the resident moonshine distributor. Dad made an arrangement with Mike to purchase a piece of property my father, in turn, purchased the property from him.

Mike would frequently run out of his stock, so he'd send dad out as well as my older brother Doug and I for a trip to get some more. The black folks made their own moonshine during this period. These types of backdoor and home-grown businesses evolved out of racism and prejudice as the black businesses developed and grew in a parallel universe to white business such as moonshiners, butcher shops whether the businesses were legal or illegal. It was about five miles out of town, just outside of Roanoke and Dad did this before I can remember, during the entire time I lived at home with my family. As time went on, I didn't feel like going on any more trips when I turned fourteen, I was thinking about girls, but especially—baseball.

In less than twenty years on the farm, my parents had nine children: six girls and three boys, I was the youngest, named, Larry Edwin LeGrande, born May 25, 1939 and raised on their country farm. The farm was additional income for the family and kept us fed as we did our fair share working on the farm tending the animals and working the crops. The stability provided from the railroad gave us all an unchanging environment for decades to our adulthood. All the children attended the local, segregated school in Salem, Virginia, that was in walking distance from our farm.

Courtesy of Pat Davis.
Dad, L. S. Legrande clutching young Larry.

In 1941, as war raged in Europe, defense industries boomed in the United States. However, while hundreds of thousands of whites found jobs in the defense industries, only a few thousand blacks were hired as porters, janitors and other menial jobs. Most of defense employers refused to hire black workers no matter how skilled they were. Some blacks took it upon themselves to do something to make a change, so black leaders decided that black workers should conduct a march at the White House until the President opened up jobs for blacks. Roosevelt finally agreed to meet with the, then recently-formed NAACP. They told him that they wanted him to integrate the army and forbid discrimination and segregation in defense industries. Roosevelt compromised and decided not to integrate the army but he would ban racial discrimination in industry.

While my father continued to work for the railroad, his sideline job was running moonshine "corn liquor" in Franklin County—the moonshine capital at the time. My Dad was pretty slick back then. Dad, in trying to avoid prying eyes, would go to the stills and get half gallon jars and put them in a suitcase. He would take me and my brother Doug with him as decoys for the police. We would sit on the back seat with our feet on the suitcase and he would drive thirty miles an hour with a trail of cars behind him beeping at him to speed up, but he took his time with us in the car so he wouldn't be obvious; much like going for a Sunday drive in the country.

My brother, who was five years my senior, helped in the storage for Dad's personal stash of "shine" in the basement after a trip from the mountains. Dad had a homemade cabinet about three foot off the floor with a lock on it. Brother Doug, one day figured out that he could take a screwdriver and work some magic on dad's "shine" enclosure. He said, "Larry, come down here and hold the door—keep it steady!" Doug unscrewed the hinge with the lock still in tact. We laughed and got excited because we felt like we had just struck gold! After we swore secrecy, we poured a pint with a Coca-Cola. We sampled goods, undetected for about seven years. One day when I was about seventeen years old, I had sampled too much and ended up lying on the bed holding onto the headboard. The bed was turning over like an alligator in a spin-roll. Pretty soon I hit the floor. My mother found out I was sick, and of course, told Dad. When Dad finally caught us, we got a hefty, but justifiable beating.

As a young boy, I learned the ways of hard work, respect and integrity. Except for my lapse in judgment with dad's moonshine—it was all Doug's fault. My daily chores of working in the hog pens, chicken pens, and garden rows took hours to complete. By weeks end, I was exhausted from all the work and sought some relief in play. My redemption was to know that Saturday was all mine—baseball from sun up to sun down. But before playing, I had to do all my chores and did so early, I had to wake up the rooster. I spent my Sundays at church with the family. We, as young adults, were not taught to drive, so we walked to school or wherever we needed to go. I was the youngest of eight children. My mother had a baby girl after me, but she didn't live to see her first birthday. The homestead was very old and small at the time. My father had added onto the house as the children were added to our family so we ended up with four bedrooms upstairs and three downstairs. It seemed like constant construction growing up in this house.

Although I once tried to change into my play clothes after returning from church to squeeze in some afternoon baseball—that didn't work all too well. I quickly learned that by doing so, I made myself available for doing chores at the farm. From that point forward, I stayed dressed in my Sunday best all day long—as often as I could get away with it! At nine years of age, my brother would pitch to me and when we had a chance, gathered for the neighborhood games and it continued for five years. I had built my strength and physique by farming and hard labor as well as digging post holes in the ground. My childhood baseball memories today have been plucked from broomsticks, homemade baseballs and makeshift ballfields. I had baseball fever and it would remain with me the rest of my days.

The Grafleys were our next door neighbors. They must have loved baseball as much as the rest of us to let land go unproductive—except for the pure pleasure of the game. They would always let us use their field to play. We had a sickle and cut back most of their yard to play. We used broomsticks for bats and rocks for bases. When the broomsticks broke, I simply went out in the woods with an axe and cut off a limb thirty inches long and when that broke, I cut another. With mom making hand-made baseballs and nature supplying the rest, equipment to play ball was never exhausted.

Courtesy of Pat Davis. Larry as a little boy.

The Grafleys would also allow local small town teams to play on their field. These teams would drive up to a half hour to play on their field. When these teams showed up, they would bring their own re-stitched sacks filled with sawdust that they had cut down to size from farm-animal feedsacks to use for their bases and had their own bats and real baseballs. Because there was no backstop and no fences at the time, all the kids competitively ran down the foul balls or home runs and were paid 50 cents for each ball retrieved. I'd always watch these teams play—day and night when I could—this is when

I caught baseball fever. And after all the hitting instruction from my brother Doug, and watching these games, I said to myself, I can play this game!

So with my enthusiastic stride, I approached the home team called the "Pinkard Court Wolves" one day, and asked them if I could warm up the pitcher. They let me catch! Then I thought…I'll ask them if I could take batting practice with them. Again, they obliged. Once they saw how hard I could throw, catch and how well I could hit, Robert "Genie" Simmons came up to visit Dad and asked if I could play with them. Dad responded, "That's alright, just don't let him get hurt!" Robert, replied, "Ok! We WON'T let him get hurt!" Robert and I knew that he just told Dad what he wanted to hear, so I could play ball. I was only fourteen years old at the time, and they were no younger than twenty-six and most of them in their 30's. Robert, who played for the Wolves, transitioned me from watching and practicing with the Wolves to playing with the Webster All-Stars.

The Red Sox had a minor league team in Roanoke in the 1950's as well. When they were in town playing their home games, the newspaper and the radio would build my excitement and drive my passion to attend. I would get up at the crack of dawn, bust my ass to feed the chickens and slop the hogs, knock out all my chores and make Dad or Doug take me as often as we could to the local minor league Red Sox games. Going to these games was the highlight of my entire month, despite having to sit way out on the grass down the third base line pouring rain or shine. While the white folks sat sheltered under the covered stadium.

I didn't mind about the little things. I didn't care about the weather, or that I'd be sitting in the mud for hours or that the white folks were under the cover of the stadium. My excitement just being at the game was good enough for me—bar none!

Going to these games kept my baseball fever at a high pitch and fueled my dreams!

As World War II began in 1939 and lasted for over five years, most of the million or more black soldiers who enlisted in the armed services knew that they would serve in segregated units and mostly in non-combat jobs. Many of the war veterans returned to their homes after the war as farmers. The veterans learned from their parents as they returned home with a warning to them, that if authorities found photos of white women with black soldiers, whether they were photos of friends or employers they would be hunted down, arrested and possibly killed. Yet another chilling glimpse into the violence that African Americans faced in the Jim Crow era of the South. Jim Crow, a fictional character, embodies the era of intense segregation and hatred between the whites and blacks during the early to mid-nineteenth century. Thus, black players formed their own units, black sports teams, leagues and "barnstorming" around the country to play anyone who would challenge them. On and off the field, athletes faced the sting of bigotry, no matter what age, or sex, racism was in its peak. They were facing an irrevocable past and an uncertain future.

At the age of fourteen, I was behind the plate catching for the local Webster All-Stars, an all-Negro semi-professional industrial team of Blue Ridge in Virginia. A brick manufacturing company sponsored the team. Most of the teammates were grown men ten to fifteen years older. The next youngest on the team was twenty-six years old. Baseball was not offered at our Carver School; however, they did have basketball and football of which I availed myself to the football team. The local little league teams at the time were so deeply segregated that black children were not allowed to play with white children. So my teammates and I continued to play in our fields and work on the farm.

As history was trying to mature itself from the bounds of segregation, the judicial system turned its eye to social reform. The 1954 United States Supreme Court decision in *Oliver L. Brown et. al. v. the Board of Education of Topeka, Kansas* is among the most significant judicial turning points in the development of our country that had dismantled the legal basis for racial segregation in schools and other public buildings. This guaranteed all citizens' equal protection of laws and that discrimination or racial segregation violated the 14th amendment to the United States Constitution. This decision not only affected the educational system but social reform and catapulted the Civil Rights Movement along with our dearly departed Martin Luther King. Although, it did not abolish segregation in other public areas, such as restaurants and restrooms nor did it require desegregation of public schools, the iron hand of oppression would offer continuing racial atrocities for several more years to come.

In the mid-1950s, less than half of the United States population had television sets and anything that was broadcast was in black and white for those that could afford one. By the time my parents did get a television set I was well on my way to practicing every chance I had with my brother Doug and watching any highlights of the major league games on television.

In the dusky path of what seemed like a dream, spring arrived as a heated blanket in 1957 and the Memphis Red

Sox had come to play a game with the Birmingham Black Barons in Salem, Virginia.

Homer "Goose" Curry and his team were at a local restaurant, close by. As they were leaving the restaurant and getting back on the bus to drive to the municipal field, Goose initiated a conversation with a gentleman bypasser, named Robert "Butters" Lewis. He happened to be out for a stroll in front of the restaurant when Goose inquired if there were any good, black baseball players in the area. Butters responded that he knew of one…and that was me! Butters in turn, called my folks and told them that, "They need to get me to the game tonight because the manager of the team wants to talk to me about playing in the Negro Leagues!" So, my brother Doug, took me to the game that evening. We didn't even need tickets to get in, because I told the people at the ticket gate that the manager wanted to talk to me about playing in the league. They didn't believe me at first so they watched us go all the way into the dugout and I finally made them believe and didn't they charge us the ticket fee to get in. Butters had watched me play numerous times on the Webster's All-Stars and if it wasn't for him, I would have never come off the farm and would have remained in Roanoke, Virginia.

One of my interviews with *The Roanoke Times* in 1997 sums it up, "One spring day in 1957 the Memphis Red Sox, a Negro American League Team, and their shrewd, tough-fisted manager, Homer "Goose" Curry, came to Salem to play an exhibition game at Municipal Field. 'They were parked in the street in Salem, LeGrande recalls. And this black man walked passed. His name was Butters Lewis. Goose Curry asked him if he knew of any black baseball players. And he told him he knew of one—and his name was Larry LeGrande.' "[4]

I was a young athletic catcher for the Webster All-Stars when the Negro League noticed me and plucked me out of the deep country fields of Virginia. Many, many, thanks again to Butters Lewis!

Then next thing I know, Dad gave me a train pass to go from Roanoke to Memphis. My mother happily cooked two pullets, baked several biscuits and packed apples for the long two-day trip that was approximately 700 miles away. CBS debuted *"Leave it to Beaver"*, but I never saw the series until my latter years.

I thought about making this very long, lonely Memphis journey. My decision to go was certainly my destiny, since one more summer in the hog pens would be unbearable. I had my practice arm ready from working in the hog pens, slinging buckets of water and food and felt very confident that I could make this team.

Salem, Virginia always had a large interest in athletics. This fanaticism not only brought the interest of a minor league team and eventually Negro League barnstorming for the city's economy, but also produced that fantastic moment in time where the alignment of Homer "Goose" Curry, "Butters" Lewis and finally, my destiny came to fruition.

The city today hosts a number of other statewide, regional, and national sporting events at its facilities. It has been the home of the Salem Red Sox, a Class-A affiliate of the Boston Red Sox. The Amos Alonzo Stagg Bowl, NCAA Division III Football Championship game is also held at the Salem Football Stadium. The NCAA Men's Division III Basketball Championship and the NCAA Division III Volleyball Championship came to the Salem Civic Center as well as the Women's NCAA Division III Softball Championship to Moyer Field. In 2007, the Salem Football Stadium also hosted the annual Southwestern Virginia Educational Classic. Salem High School has also become well-known for its athletic programs, especially the football team which has proudly won six state championships since 1996.

Although, I was happy, overwhelmed, excited and not knowing what was around the corner in my life, this trip took on a whole new outlook. It was a bitter-sweet time for my family, who were happy, but my parents feared my leaving home by myself. As I look back, it must have been an incredibly scary time for them. I'd be traveling through the countryside on a train, making many stops with strangers getting on and off the train. It was a huge risk, but when you're young you have no fear and I had no understanding of the great, bad beyond. The adults in my life would continue to ask me if 'I was sure' and if 'I still wanted to make a trip like that all by myself', but the answer stayed the same—OH YES, SIR! YES, MA'AM!

High School—
Turning The Page

I was forced by segregation to attend Carver High School in Salem, Virginia. All of my brothers and sisters attended this school as well. Principal Chauncey Harmon was a stern, but understanding man. He was principal of Carver High School from 1953 to 1966. I wasn't nervous about asking to see the Principal, so when I saw that he wasn't busy talking to anyone I ran into his office and said, "Principal Harmon! I have something very important to ask you!" He said, "Sit down son, what's your question?" As I caught my breath from the hallway sprint, I said, "Principal Harmon, can I be excused from school for three weeks? I've been asked to baseball tryouts as a catcher and outfielder and I'll be taking the train to Memphis. Is it ok if I go? I'll keep up with my studies!" He said, "If it's ok with your parents, then it's ok by me! Of Course!" Principal Harmon allowed me to leave school temporarily with the promise to return and finish my studies. Nothing beats education because you will need it before and after sports. You had to have a place to work, and could not depend on the money in sports. You could get hurt, or worse. Mr. Harmon loved sports and knew my ability. He had seen me play baseball as well as football and knew my talent was one of the best in the entire school.

I had just started my senior year in high school, and I was almost 18 years old when I asked Mr. Harmon if I could be excused with my promise to return and finish my studies and graduate. I had the lead in my high school play at the time and agreed that I would study and memorize my lines during this three week absence from school. *"Of course!"*, was the answer, those two words rang in my head for days and my excitement was building for the tryouts. Knowing my character as well as my promise to keep up with my grades, he gracefully approved.

When considering this particular sports career, I would say it depends on what organization you are in, who likes you and dislikes you, the scout that signs you—he has to stick with you. I had Jerry Coleman, second baseman for the New York Yankees in my day. After Coleman graduated from high school, he then spent his entire playing career with the New York Yankees. He played six years in their minor league system before reaching the big club in 1949. Coleman hit .275 in his first year and led all second basemen in fielding percentage. He won the Associated Press' Rookie of the Year Award in 1949. Coleman's career declined after he was injured the following season, relegating him to the bench. He was forced to retire after the 1957 season, but left on good footing; hitting .364 in a World Series loss against the Milwaukee Braves. He appeared in the World Series six times in his career, winning four of them. The scouts have a big influence on college education for potential players.

Back in the day, when the New York Yankees made increasingly more revenues, they started to send their men to college and paid for everything. The Kansas City Athletics (now known as the Oakland Athletics) made it their priority to send their players to college. The other teams followed suit. They wanted to send you to college after you sign, because they liked good, intelligent players. I believe Oakland had won the World Series because they had the best strategic ball players such as Reggie Jackson, Mark McGuire, Dave Stewart, Mike Norris, Jose´ Conseco, Dave Henderson and Rickey Henderson. They had a good team and were backed by a good organization.

Education is important because it helps with understanding the strategy in the game, and contracts are crucial at the time of negotiations, neither of which I had much of. Agents work the bargaining and negotiations and you certainly need to understand what you're facing in terms of third parties planning your career, your life and making money on your abilities and intellect. They hold your life in their hands, their heads—good or bad.

I was a little black boy that would be leaving home for a few weeks for baseball tryouts. I gave no thought of strangers kidnapping me or even a brush with the KKK. I only knew that I would have food, shelter and safety when I got there, as my parents told me that I would. Beyond that—it was all about the tryouts—nothing more. This was going to be my ticket to my next life and the farm would be history. I had no interest in becoming a farmer, raising cattle or even being in the moonshine trade.

All I could think of was going to the tryouts and showing them that I could play with the best of 'em. I was going to get that clean, white, uniform and prove to my parents and the high school that I was a great ballplayer and it was going to happen real soon.

Looking back, my parents were making a tough choice. They hoped they weren't making the wrong choice. What if I had failed? What if I'd never returned home? What if? It must have been a difficult decision for them to make. Most parents want the best for their kids and they knew I was very good at baseball, but no one knew just how good.

For me, my attitude was just as important as my ability. I knew I could show the scouts what I could do. I had in my possession one of life's greatest gifts and that was natural talent.

Tryouts and Negotiations
with the "Goose"

The train ride was long and lonely. I arrived in Memphis, feeling apprehensive and frightened, but overall very anxious and excited. After all, I had never been away from the farm in my seventeen years. Homer met me at the train station and said, "Here I am boy!" We proceeded to the great Martin's Stadium on Crump Boulevard. When we pulled up, standing there, bigger than life itself, was two of the biggest players I had ever seen and they were trying out for the team as well. Of course, my first thought was to be very competitive:—beat them—no matter the price. They proceeded to inform me that "As small as you are, boy, you're gonna get killed!" Since I was only 5'9" and 159 pounds, size did not matter to me, I knew I had the skill and I was intent on proving it.

The try-outs included eighty-six people; however, there were only twenty-one uniforms available, and…most of them were already picked for the team. As try-outs proceeded, we had to sprint from the left-field line to the right-field line. When they said, "Go!" Sam Allen from Norfolk, Virginia took off like a bat out of hell and I was right on his heels. He came in first and I came in second place in that sprint race out of eighty-six people—I was sure happy about that. Sam and I had a real good laugh because two Virginia boys took the top two spots in the race. After the race, we took infield practice. When it was my time to shine, the coach had me throw down to second base and I made *"THE"* perfect throw—6" to the first base side of the bag and 6" off the ground. The coach expected perfection—and they got it! The coach, in disbelief, said, "Throw down again!" And again they were amazed—lightening struck twice—another perfect throw.

The feeling I had was indescribable and made it through the try-outs at the famous Martin Stadium in Memphis Tennessee and "Goose" Curry was all smiles from ear to ear. For me, there was no turning back to the farm—the cattle, the pigs, the chickens and the crop fields. I felt like I was finally at my home away from home.

I knew I made a good impression because "Goose" picked me up the following day, and said, "Let's take a ride to the hospital!" to talk about my first contract with Dr. Martin, one of the owners of Martin Stadium. *I felt big! I felt proud!* Finally the good Lord blessed me—He was taking me out of the weeds, stick bats and mudfields. Moreover, there was no opportunity for the blacks to play little league baseball and no high school team. *I was ready to play real baseball with real players! I had made the team after a three-week try-out!* Wow! I was just a seventeen-year old kid and I was getting one of the twenty-one uniforms! *I felt like I just slayed those two Goliaths that threatened this small boy the day before!*

Martin's Stadium was one of a kind back in the day. This was a place where the Negro players could "stay 'n play". There were efficiency apartments and rooms located under the left-field seats at the stadium for each player to live in at night and play ball by day. I was overwhelmed by the stadium's architecture; Goose told me that the place was way ahead of its time and most certainly unique. The other stadiums didn't have a built-in rooms for the players. The Martin's ensured our safety as well. It was a lot like an enclosed compound just for us black players with no threats from the outside.

Because segregation was extremely prominent in most baseball fields, the Martin's Stadium was built and housed for the black athletic community without restrictions. The most popular players that emerged from the Memphis Red Sox was pitcher, Satchel Paige and their outfielder, James "Cool Papa" Bell, as well as Charley Pride.

Courtesy of Dr. Layton Revel, CNLBR. Printed with permission.
Original Martin's Stadium. Memphis, Tennessee

The Martins were at the center of the Medical District in the area of Crump Boulevard. Numerous hospitals, clinics, dental practices and sanatoriums were built in the early 19th century in this area. Beale Street became one of the more popular areas for music and entertainers. The franchise was owned by four Martin brothers W. S., J. B., A. T., and B. B.; two of which operated the franchise and were also dentists, Dr. J. B. Martin and Dr. B. B. Martin. Dr. J. B. Martin operated a drugstore, a funeral home and also invested in real estate. They also owned a hotel next to the baseball park. On occasion they would operate the concession stand where they would serve chitterlings as part of the ballpark menu as well as the standard fare of popcorn, peanuts, hotdogs and hamburgers.

*Memphis Red Sox Owners outside South Memphis
Drug Company on Florida Street*

*Reprinted with permission. Memphis and Shelby County
Room, Memphis Public Library & Information Center*

*The men standing in suits were the owners of the Memphis-based
black baseball team known as the Memphis Red Sox. The Hooks
brothers, Martin Brothers and others were the principal owners.
These distinguished gentlemen from Memphis, TN were the proud
owners of a competitive black baseball team in Memphis.*

Memphis at the time was emerging as the country or "sharecropper" music capital of this country. There was less than a half million people at the time, but it seemed bigger than life with musicians, shops and barbers with a great social atmosphere. It was clean, mostly safe and beautiful. We were considered to be in the Deep South or the Mississippi delta area. The kings of country, rock and roll and blues emerged from this musical area with well-known artists such as Johnny Cash, B.B. King and of course Elvis Presley in the 1950's. Charley Pride who also played for the Memphis Red Sox also emerged from this famous city later on to embark on his music career. Blues, Jazz and Gospel music was floating through the streets everywhere I walked, day and night—music would be soaring out through the pool halls and nightclubs.

Walking down any of these streets you would see the structures in early nineteenth century Italianate, Greek and Second Empire. These Victorian-style homes were ornate mansions that would tower above your eyes. The smaller, more modest homes were much like little cottages, some with a little grass and a white pickett fence in the front yard.

A couple of years after I left Memphis, urban renewal began in the 1960's and ran through the late 1970's so quickly that people referred this razing of buildings as the white tornado. Some feared that their home, place of business or building would be knocked down at a moment's notice. The razing happened so rapidly it eliminated many of the historical sites without a second thought to their future value.

Homer "Goose" Curry, was first manager I ever had and of course the first Negro team I played on with Memphis. Goose was known for inventing the hook shot, or the skyhook in his basketball tenure, this shot became famous with Kareem Abdul-Jabbar. Goose was 6' 1" tall, so his shots were like throwing change in the church basket—easy. He accompanied me to the Memphis Hospital to talk to Dr. W. S. Martin, the owner of the Memphis Red Sox. Mr. Martin was one of the very well-to-do doctors who owned the stadium. 'Goose' told me on the way, "Let me do all the talking." We arrived at the hospital office where Mr. Martin was waiting for us. Mr. Martin said to me, "Take a seat outside." But as I waited outside, I had given an ear to the demon of false glory. I overheard 'Goose' say, "Doc, he's a really good ballplayer, ya need ta pay him $250.00 a month." Doc said, "I can't give him $250.00 a month! Send him back, it's just too much." Goose retorted, "I think we should pay him$200.00 a month". Doc responded, "Well, ya gotta pay him somethin'. Pay him $200.00 on the fifteenth of every month." Doc replied, "Well, he's a good boy, we can sell this contract and make money off him, just like we sold Bob Boyd".

When I returned to my room, I told my teammates about the deal and they said, "That dirty bastard!" Some said, they had been playing over twenty-five years and didn't get this kind of pay. Many were in the Negro Leagues for some length of time, because some were ex-convicts, some were pretty mean if they were 'messed with'. So nobody really bothered us, we didn't let outsiders take advantage of us. They had played baseball in prison, they were the 'tough guys'—the enforcers of the teams. But it was the best-kept secret—some of these guys had some bad histories. No one talked about them very much, but I saw them as really good players, and usually a foot taller than I was! People still came from miles around unbeknownst to the public that some of the players were criminals. People sat in trees waiting to see us play, but especially, more importantly, to see Satchel.

Following this financial windfall that I overheard the day before, it was the next morning, when 'Goose' knocked on my door and said, "Come to the kitchen, Larry!" We then stepped next door into the dressing room where 'Goose' started to count out a stash of cash on the rubbing table. He ran his hand in his pocket and counts out $175.00 in one-dollar ($1.00) bills, although I wasn't counting, I was staring at all that green. The more he counted, the more I smiled...it was my very first pay out. This was the essence of my lack of negotiation skills and education. But it was the most money I had ever had and I earned it. It was almost top dollar for the 'famous Negro Leagues'. By today's standards it was worth around $4,000.00 a month, I thought this was good money. I made the team...and did not get cut! *I WAS BIG TIME!* As the year went on, big time meant that we dressed sharp every day, got paid for having fun and it was heaven on earth! I had left the farm. I was traveling the United States and I was getting paid to play baseball.

I noticed it was a heck of pile of money-it had to be at least five inches thick! 'Goose' says, "Ya! See boy? I told ya I'd get ya some money." He left, and I proceeded to count the money only to find there was only $175.00, not $250.00, not even $200.00 like I had overheard the day before. Thus, was my first induction into the big bad world. Goose was a thief—he cheated me, but he got me in the famous Negro Leagues, so I couldn't fault him too much.

Talent and Character is Put To The Test—My Red Sox Debut

The Memphis Red Sox was a professional Negro League baseball team based in Memphis, Tennessee, from the 1920s until the end of segregated baseball. The Memphis Red Sox played in the Negro National League for most of the League's existence, although they also played independently, in the Negro Southern League, before becoming members of the Negro American League in 1937. They had their greatest success in 1938, when they won the Negro American League first half with a 21–4 record. One of the Memphis Red Sox's players was the country western singer, Charley Pride. What an honor it was to be around him!

Opening day competition was with the Birmingham Black Barons. This was Willie Mays' team before he signed with the Giants.

The following week, the schedule called for the Memphis Red Sox to go to Birmingham to play the Black Barons. There I was in Birmingham, Alabama for the first time with my first team bus ride. As the boys filed out of their dressing rooms and into the dugout, I was shocked; I thought to myself, I've never seen so many black people in my life in one spot. This stadium proved to be more crowded than our home field—15,000 strong!

It was game time. I was scared to death when the place started filling up. I was used to about 1,000 fans in the stadium, this time, it seemed like the whole city was going to be watching! My small town school never prepared for me for this!

I unconsciously walked into the dressing room and proceeded to stay in the bathroom, and did not want to come back out. The coach found me and asked, "Where you been boy!?" I said, "I have been in the bathroom." The coach barked out, "We need you to go to the bullpen and warm up the pitcher." I froze. He smiled at me and said, "Let's Go!" With that great, comforting smile, I headed to the bullpen...but I was still scared to death. I had never seen so many people in my life. When I returned to the dugout, sitting there that day, I dugout that day, I felt I had finally made it with some of the big boys like my idol, Willie Mays. Sitting, watching and waiting. The sounds of the fans were getting louder and louder, the smell of food stronger and stronger. I should have been excited and pumped as hell. Suddenly, unexplained anxiety took over—I was scared to death—I wished I was back in my hometown of Roanoke. The nervous anxiety must have lasted over an hour as I sat and waited for the coach to call my name into action. He said, "I want you to go up and pinch hit for the pitcher to lead off the inning."

My stage fright made a surprise comeback. This time, it was so fierce I automatically got up and left the dugout. I sat in the dressing room, quietly and looked at some of the baseballs and bats that were scattered. My courage slowly returned. When I finally got the nerve to come back out, I slowly sauntered to the plate. The coach barked at me again, "Next time I ask you to get up there, you'd better listen!"

I walked to the plate and stared straight ahead. I was focused and concentrated as hard as I could…but I stood there—paralyzed as the first pitch came in for a strike. My teammates immediately starting yelling at me from the dugout—"Get ready out there!" The next pitch was a perfect fast-ball on the outside corner which I took for strike two. Now I was down 0–2. I knew I had to guard the plate on the next pitch. The third pitch I was ready to swing when the pitcher threw a curve-ball that I unceremoniously popped out to the second baseman. I put the ball in play, *BUT* I felt like I belonged because I made contact with the pitch! As I continued to play the game, it got a little better and my fear of crowds finally disappeared. My batting average was well over .300 for the Memphis Red Sox. I thought back to my paltry, local audience in the Virginia days. I heard my name being shouted, the anguish disappeared and by the time I hit the ball, my focus was second to none.

One of the most fascinating and rare occurrences with one of these baseball players was Charley Pride's ability to play baseball and sing, and boy, could he sing!. He finally crossed over into country music with the help of Chet Atkins. I always was amazed at how he became so famous in spite of all the racial challenges that were all around us. Charley embarked on his singing career in country music after he put down his glove. He was country music's first black singing superstar. But I remember that before hitting the big times in Nashville, Pride was a tremendous pitcher with a great knuckleball. Pride was always practicing for his next career. He would sing on the bus, in the locker rooms and in the showers—he sang and toted his guitar everywhere. Charley sang country music. We don't know how he ever got into singing country, but we had to listen to it anyway even though the rest of us preferred Blues and Jazz. Our number one Blues tune in black music then, was "The Things That I Used to Do", by Guitar Slim.

Charley and I went on to become friends, partly because of the seating arrangements on the bus, even until present day. The seating arrangement was a peculiar thing. I got on the bus for the first time. There was an empty seat right in front of Charley Pride. Little did I know, this was always going to be my seat. Everyone sat in the seats they had picked for the remainder of the season. Nobody would take another person's seat, with one exception: Poker nights on the bus! This caused a seat shuffle with some of the team members to gather around the makeshift card table.

The Memphis Red Sox also played against the Anderson Falstaffs, one of today's long-forgotten teams. The Falstaffs based out of Anderson, Indiana was a formidable team. We played on a hot summer's day in August of 1957. *The Anderson Herald* writes, "Memphis, current leader in the Negro American League, is led by Lonnie Harris, a centerfielder and leading base stealer in the circuit; Albert Strozier, shortstop and starter of the most double plays in the loop; Rufus Gibson, second baseman; Isaac Barnes, first baseman and home-run hitter; James Valintine, third baseman; Eugene Roberts, left-fielder; and Larry LeGrande, right-fielder."[12] Falstaffs boasted an interesting history from their namesake of Falstaff beer. Beer companies would own and/or manage some of the baseball teams with an extra added advantage of promoting their beer through sports teams. The Falstaffs were one of the first ones to accomplish this venue and their brand.

Lonnie "Showboat" Harris was so talented, he ended up playing in the Negro Leagues for eight seasons and played for the mighty Birmingham Black Barons. He went on to join the U. S. Army and play in two East-West All-Star games.

For the greater part of the Memphis Red Sox history, the team was owned by J. B. Martin and B.B. Martin of Memphis, brothers who both maintained dental practices and other business enterprises as well as other investors. J. B. Martin owned the Chicago Giants. A third brother, W. S. Martin owned the Red Sox Franchise and soon became president of the Negro League. The brothers had other businesses such as running the local hospital and built Martin Park on Crump Boulevard, making their Memphis Red Sox one of the few clubs in the Negro Leagues with their own ballpark. It seemed they left no stone unturned to make money.

Charley Pride   Larry Le Grande

Larry LeGrande. Photo of Charley Pride, country singer and Larry LeGrande.

A few years back, in 2000, the Negro Leagues had a reunion to remember—there were about 200 players that attended. It took place in Kansas City, Missouri. I was always so very honored to be acquainted with Charley. Charley always mentioned to everyone that I could throw the ball with the best of the best.

Nobody ever got long-term contracts in the Negro Leagues. They were always one-year contracts we needed to prove ourselves year after year. When I was with Memphis, in 1957, the team took a trip to Comiskey Park in Chicago for the All-Star Negro Leagues. They were held there most of the time. Later on, they had them in New York and in Kansas City.

Here I was in the best seat of the house, watching the best players in the world on a beautiful hot summer day in Chicago. Life was very, very good for an eighteen-year old boy from a farm in Roanoke—destiny made an appearance at the game and made its way to my seat. Ted Raspberry walked by and I quickly jumped to my feet—and stopped him. He was a sharp dressed man who carried a briefcase, sported a suit and alligator shoes, a very rich man. He was very serious, almost never taking his eyes off the ballfield and his players. As my question came flying out at Mr. Raspberry, I asked, "Could I come to spring training with your team next year?" To my surprise, he said, "You sure can!" My first thought was he was full of shit, 'cus they'd often say this and never call back. He took my contact information, and my first phone number at the time was 26785. The months rolled by, and by spring, I got the call. He sent the bus ticket and I was on my way to spring training for the Detroit Stars.

In reflecting on this, I remember that there were over 20,000 people there and I believe God placed me there in the stands just so I could talk to Ted Raspberry and he would become the man to launch my professional ball-playing career. I could have been on the other side of the stadium, but there I was, behind home plate and I came face to face with him. I had asked him that golden question.

When the 1957 season was over, I had no money to return home on the train back to Roanoke. Understandably, it was my first taste of real money, independence as a late teenager. I had experienced Beal Street on my personal time away from the stadium. The culture, the food, the music—and the women— it was like being in a rich man's dream. They air was full of distant strains of old songs. The women's perfume saturating the night with wild fragrances. Everyone was always smiling and laughing as they walked down Beal Street.

I had spent *all* of my money having fun. Although I went from one night club to another I was still too young to buy alcohol, but that didn't stop me. Meanwhile, back home, my family was trying to scrape up some money to send me for the return and the long ride back, but I had to wait a couple of weeks before my envelope would arrive.

Dr. Martin had set up deals with the Traveler's Hotel whereby the visiting teams would stay when they were in town. A local wealthy woman owned the hotel, and since she got great business from this arrangement, I was allowed to stay at the Traveler's Hotel for free for the two weeks until my envelope arrived. This Hotel, by the way, was just a couple blocks away from the Lorraine Hotel where we eventually lost our beloved Dr. Martin Luther King, Jr.

There was a local, black restaurant where the home team and visiting teams frequented. When spring training started and throughout the season, the waitresses would anticipate a bonanza as the team players came in for their food and drink. After each season, their money WAS IN THE BANK! When I told the restaurant owner of my situation, despite knowing I had blown all my money on Beal Street, they let me eat for free until it was time to return to Roanoke.

I didn't grow up believing that where I was on the farm—that's where I was going to be. I knew in my heart, I was going to become something greater.

I've always believed that talent is inherent and I knew I had that naturally. I had developed my skill in hours and hours on the farm and hours and hours in practice. I would show a desperate, obsessive focus with every fiber of my being to be successful. I was doing what I loved, I wasn't doing it to make money, but I knew the money would follow.

My parents were happy—they were proud, but they knew I didn't know how to handle money. It was my first taste of real money and a good time on Beal Street night after night. After all, most of us do crazy things when we're young, and I was no different. I would still return to my loving family who took me back in with open arms, laughter and a pat on the back. My brothers and sisters always needed something to pick on, so the laughs rolled in when they found out I blew all of my money in the big city.

In 1957, Hank Aaron came on the scene with the Milwaukee Braves, in the Major Leagues, most news coverage would be all about the New York Yankees. He won the NL MVP Award with a .322 batting average 132 RBI and 44 home runs. They went on to win the pennant that year and defeated the Yankee team in the World Series 4–3, he hit .393 with three home runs in the seven game series.

The Milwaukee Braves defeated the New York Yankees, but I was still faithful to the Yankees. It was also the peak of the baby boomers as hundreds of thousands of service personnel returned home from their military tours. And Martin Luther King had started his nationwide tour to speak on segregation and oppression.

The unions were very active mostly in the north where the Teamsters union were expelled from the AFL-CIO for failing to deal with organized crime. Jimmy Hoffa was President of the Teamsters and not only played a major role in the development of the union, but was also a big civil rights supporter and made it known in his speeches and in the media.

In the United States, the Civil Right Act was enacted. This helped to ensure that the black vote would be counted. In the South, the apathy still raged on and many blacks were coerced not to vote and some didn't bother to take advantage of this liberty under the intimidation and oppression that continued. Although it increased the overall black vote, if anyone was caught obstructing the black registered voter there would be a trial by jury. However, the entire jury would be all whites as blacks were not allowed to be jurors at the time.

The Detroit Stars

I had debuted with the Memphis Red Sox in 1957 and moved on to the Detroit Stars in 1958. I was thrilled to get on the Detroit Stars team because they traveled a lot more than the Memphis Red Sox—I was going to get more exposure to scouts. I was also going to get more playing time because I knew I should be playing every day. A couple of different sports writers and news reporters had described me as being compared to Willie Mays. *The Morning Herald* out of Maryland reported, "The Negro American League comes to town tonight when the Memphis Red Sox and the Detroit Stars clash beneath the Municipal Stadium arcs at 8 o'clock". They went on to say, "Other Detroit players who will bear special watching are fast-ball pitcher Will Harris and catcher-outfielder, Larry LeGrande. A 16-year old from Jacksonville, Florida who resembles Willie Mays when the San Francisco star was starting out".[16]

I believe my best all-around game ever played was with the 1958 Detroit Stars against the Birmingham Black Barons in Birmingham, Alabama. This was the stadium where Willie Mays would pack the house seven years earlier and it was still packed seven years later with these loyal fans as I entered the stadium. I believe this was the best baseball city I had ever played in because of their love, loyalty and enthusiasm and it permeated throughout the stadium. It was standing room only, with all the black fans relegated to the upper deck in right field and they were turning fans away as they attempted to enter. I was playing right-field and leading off. I went 2 for 3 that day with 2 singles and an RBI. I threw a runner out at the plate from right-field, and I made the game-saving catch at the right-field corner at the fence off the bat of Eugene "Stanky" White. We won 4–3! We were at a homefield disadvantage, with umpire calls leaning and crowds rooting for the other team—here we were celebrating after beating one of the best teams in the league. My teammates were on the field, jumping and hootin' and hollerin' and my teammates started to wonder why I wasn't joining in the festivities. As I made the game-saving catch, my foot got wedged under the right-field fence and I couldn't get out to join them, until some of my teammates came out to rescue me from clutches of the wire fencing.

In the Negro Leagues the umpires would usually call the games 'straight', but the home field advantage gave the umpires the liberty to lean towards the home team with their calls. In this game with the Barons, they called it straight because our manager, Ed Steele was from Birmingham. And if they didn't call it straight, they had to deal with him and he wasn't about to take any of their crap.

One very hot, muggy day in July, the Detroit Stars were playing the Birmingham Black Barons at the Columbus,

Ohio's Jet Stadium. Ted Rasberry had renamed the team from the Detroit Stars to the Detroit Clowns with co-owner Reese "Goose" Tatum. The Detroit Club was managed by Ed Steele at the time and his goal was to regain the title lost to the Kansas City Monarchs. *The Ohio Sentinel* had stated: "The club has youth, speed, power, with such standouts as Big Bernie Porter, Bill Calloway, Marv Higgins and Larry LeGrande, a 19 year old catcher."[13] Although the Baron's Willie Smith won that game 3–0, there were 1,400 fans who were excited to see Sweetwater Clifton. The tickets for the game were only $1.25 and we intended to fill the house!

Photo courtesy of Larry LeGrande. Larry LeGrande in his authentic Satchel Paige All-Stars uniform.

The dog days of August days in 1958 brought us (the Clowns) to play the famous Kansas City Monarchs several times that month. This day, the focus was on the upcoming double-header. The announcement read, "Negro Baseball returns to Yankee Stadium on Sunday, August 17, when the Detroit Clowns meet the Kansas City Monarchs in a double header. The Clowns, led by Goose Tatum and Sweetwater Clifton, are now leading the Negro American League in team batting with a nifty .289 and are third in team fielding with a .954 average." The Monarchs were forth in team batting, .218 and second in team fielding with a .963 average. Sweetwater and had played in the National Basketball Association prior to joining the Clowns and he and Goose had also played in the Globetrotters. Not only did they have funny antics, but they were extremely talented and very entertaining for the fans who came to see them. The article went on to say, "Tops with the Clowns are the following: Leading Batsmen— Sweetwater Clifton, .440; Price West, .389; Eddie Alston, 382; Goose Tatum, 390; Bernard Porter, .344; Prince Joe Henry, .301; John Eavens, 372; Walt Wilkins, 363; Art Hampton, 350; Larry LeGrande, 342." The article ended with, "A treat for New Yorkers will be a repeat of the East-West game at Yankee Stadium on Sunday, August 31st."[35]

Yankee Stadium, on August 17, 1958, *how could a day get any better!?* The Detroit Stars (Clowns) were scheduled to play the Kansas City Monarchs in a double-header. I was one of the seven leading batsman for the Stars with an average of .342 and our leading pitcher for the Monarchs was Willie Harris with an 8–0 record. Goose Tatum and Sweetwater Clifton were ready and raring to go on this day. *The New York Age* wrote, "The Clowns have seven men who hit over the .300 mark."[17] Clifton had played two years of Class A minor league ball and was moved to Triple AAA by the Cleveland Indians before quitting to join the Globetrotters.

Our leading pitcher was John Childress who was touted as the opening-day sensation at Yankee Stadium who had pitched a 3-hitter, struck out 11 and gave up five hits. John was going in with a record of 7 wins and 1 loss and was also a major league prospect.

The New York Times wrote the next day, "The Detroit Clowns and the Kansas City Monarchs split a Negro American League double-header at the Yankee Stadium yesterday. The Monarchs won the opener, 3–2, in ten innings, and the Clowns took the seventh inning second contest, 6–4. The Clowns took a 5–0 lead in the first, three innings of the afterpiece."[18]

The following Tuesday, we defeated the Monarchs 8–2. It was a proud day even as we played the game Globetrotter-style with all of our antics. There were 2,050 fans in the bleachers looking on getting a lot of laughs. Although, as I played along with "Prince" Joe Henry things got even more heated. *The Post-Standard wrote,* "Supervising the work of plate umpire Dale Barnum, Prince Joe became "enraged" at a call and struck the umpire a heavy blow to the chest protector. Barnum, literally, chased Prince Joe out of the park. Basketball-famed Goose Tatum didn't get into the game but gave an exhibition of juggling in the middle of the seventh."

"Top fielding plays of the game were turned in by Detroit second baseman Sherwood Brewer, who went far off to his left to grab a hard grounder and toss the batter out, and the Monarchs' Willie Lee and John Self. After Brewer singled to open the Detroit ninth, Clarence King slammed a low liner to right which Lee grabbed and threw to the stretching Self to double Brewer off the bag."[34]

I was chosen to play in the East-West All-Star Game the following Sunday after our spectacular performance and win over the Monarchs I had entered the All-Star Game at Yankee Stadium with a .342 average! *We felt great!* We had defeated one of the best teams in the league, we were at the top of our game and we were ready for the All-Star Game the following weekend.

I was playing with some of the best and we were about to go up against the best of the best in the league! Not only was the All-Star Game moved from Comiskey Park, but it was moved to the "House that Ruth Built"—Yankee Stadium! I was going to set foot on the field with the likes of Babe Ruth, Lou Gehrig, and Joe DiMaggio. *What's better than cloud 9? I was on cloud 18!* The great Josh Gibson also made an All-Star appearance at Yankee Stadium, and I'd be counting the days when I'd be walking in their steps.

This was only the third time that the All-Star Game event was held at Yankee Stadium since 1933. It was one of the few years that the 1958 game would move from Comiskey Park to Yankee Stadium. *The timing couldn't have been better—I had the ultimate honor of being chosen as an All-Star.*

In the final years of the East-West games at the park would tout 52,000 spectators. Jackie Robinson threw the first pitch to start the festivities. I had shaken his hand in the dugout. What an honor and an inspiration not only for me, but for all black athletes! This was **THE** moment when he told me, "We will win eventually". I knew what he meant and winning was not about the game we were about to play.

What a thrill! Once again, I was selected for my talent! I was only twenty-one years old! I was playing center field for the East, and although the West won 8–7, the thrill of being on the field with some of these great players was incredibly exhilarating. I finished the game with one run and two hits in three at bats. *The Chicago Defender* newspaper went on to say,

"While the West was depending on speed and distance for its runs, the East took advantage of errors and wildness to bring in most of its scores. A single sacrifice and a wild throw got the east one run in the second."[14] Willie Smith, the West's starting pitcher had lofted a high fly ball and I lost it in the sun. By the time I found it, with two men on in the second, all three men had scored. The left-fielder, Don Bonner's lack of fundamentals got his ass ripped as we entered the dugout. I kept my mouth shut, as our manager Ed Steele, had flames coming out of his ears, and I didn't want to feel that burn. All I could hear as I walked on by, was Ed shouting, "As long as you been playing ball, you should know better!" In this All-Star game the West had squared the game in the eighth, the walks loaded bases and the pinch hitter Ralph Fortson cleared them with a double to right field. The negro leaguers were famous for their style of playing ball. We prided ourselves in the fundamentals of baseball over any of the white teams or leagues. We knew it, everyone knew it, so Don's lack of action to back up the center-fielder was inexcusable, but more so, it tarnished something we held in high esteem—our reputation. The winning pitcher was Pete Mumford and the losing pitcher was James Gilmore. It should have been the other way around, but that momentary lapse of If it wasn't for Don's lack of execution, cost us that game.

There we were in Yankee Stadium. *I was in Yankee Stadium!* *The New York Times* reported, "Nat (Sweetwater) Clifton's steal of home in the eight inning enabled the East to defeat the West 6–5, in the American Negro Baseball League's All-Star Game at Yankee Stadium yesterday. Clifton, who is best known for his play in the National Basketball Association, scored on a two-out double steal when Ozzie Tidmore, the West's second baseman, missed the tag on Charles Douglas.

Willie Washington of the West broke a 2–2 tie in the bottom of the fifth when he clouted a 450-footer homer, good for three runs, to right center field. In the eight, Clifton singled, sending Joe Ivory from first to third. Clifton moved to second on the throw attempting to cut down Ivory. Ivory scored the tying run on a sacrifice fly-by Gideon Jarvis which also advanced Clifton to third."[36]

Just a few years before I joined the league, Mr. Martin appointed Ted "Double Duty" Radcliffe as manager of the Chicago American Giants in 1950. He was concerned about black players joining Major League teams so he instructed Radcliffe to sign white players. The team disbanded in 1952, so this experiment in reverse integration was short-lived.

Radcliffe was the first catcher to catch for Satchel Paige in the Negro Leagues—I was the last. I proceeded to ask him why he was called "Double-Duty". He said, "I had 2 women in every town!" I remember a day when he pitched a shut out in one game and did double-duty for the team and caught the second game. Ted had an excellent throwing arm like mine, I always thought he was one of the best ballplayers of all time, although he was much older than I was he had played in six of the East-West All-Star games and had hit .376 in nine exhibition games against major leaguers. Ted was certainly a force to contend with, but like Satch he had played with him as a boy in Mobile, Alabama and they understood the fundamentals of baseball decades before I reached for the Negro Leagues.

Decades later in 2008, I was in Maryland. Once again, I'm thrilled to be reunited with Ted. This photo was taken at a banquet fund raiser for the needy in the locality. Ben E. King was the entertainer for the evening. Meeting Ben was an absolute thrill for me because half my life was spent listening to his voice over the radio waves. After the festivities, the three of us sat together and talked about baseball and the entertainment industries. What an evening! It's etched in my mind forever.

Courtesy of Larry LeGrande. Photo of Ted Radcliffe and Larry LeGrande.

The following year, Satchel called me and convinced me that I needed to go to spring training in Kansas City. I felt quite strongly about going to training, I knew in my heart that if I succeeded with the Monarchs I would surely have my friend Satchel, to back me in my endeavors. After all, I was an All-Star, but more importantly Ted and Satch recognized it.

*Courtesy of Larry LeGrande. Photo of Ben
E. King and Larry LeGrande.*

The next season, I played for the Kansas City Monarchs, leading Negro League outfielders in assists for a three consecutive seasons, because of my speed and strong, accurate throwing arm. I also honed my hitting skills over my three Negro League seasons with a .300-plus batting average. Satchel was right; I succeeded in playing for the Monarchs and he received me with open arms, preparing me for our next adventure with his All-Star team. I was finally the last catcher of the greatest pitcher. ***I Found Someone to Play With!*** It has been said that Satch is the reason why baseball players wear helmets today, Satch's dangerous fastball had an edge. He knew he had the superior raw talent of pitching. He always had an upper hand against rival batters, with a velocity of at least 90 mph or more. Baseball rumors would tout that he could pitch over 100 mph sometimes reaching as high as 105 to 110 mph.

A few years ago, I was at a baseball event in Greensboro, North Carolina with Hall of Famers: Buck O'Neil, Monte Irvin of the New York Giants, and five others. As we sat together, we discussed my friend Satch's pitching. We came to a consensus that the only person who could "pull" Satchel Paige was Hall of Famer Buck Leonard of Rocky Mount, North Carolina. This is really saying something, 'cus Satch made a lot of great hitters look bad that faced him.

The white-owned Eastern League collapsed in 1929, and the Negro National League went bankrupt in 1931. Which marked the end of the Eastern Colored League as well. It was then that Black Baseball relied on barnstorming to survive playing local teams, traveling around the countryside and playing semi-pro teams and league games even into the Canadian territory. The new Negro American League was considered a major league from 1937 to the 1950's. It was Wilkinson who signed Jackie Robinson in 1945.

Black players who were prospects often signed with Major League white teams, without regard for any contracts that may or may not have been signed with Negro Leagues. Many of the Negro league teams were getting paid in cash, there was skimming off the top, pocketing cash whenever the bookies or managers wanted or players would be shorted. Many of the semi-pro teams playing around the country would not have statistics or box scores recorded, unless a local reporter would take the time to do so. Connie Johnson, in an interview with *Public Broadcasting Atlanta* mentioned that the white teams kept records and that it was difficult to get records of the games that were played. If they jumped on the bus after the game, they didn't have a chance to get newspaper clippings. Dr. William Leuchtenburg who was also in this PBA interview, stated that "It must have been hard for the people playing at the time to think that anybody, years in the future was going to care that they were making history. And that for decades to come people would want to view what they did in the same way that they viewed the baseball being played by whites. There wasn't any evidence at the time that people were treating negro baseball in that fashion, so why should they suppose that it was worth keeping permanent record."[33] Negro League owners in the latter period who complained about this practice were in a no-win difficult situation: they could not protect their own interests without interfering with the advancement of players into the white majors. Most times all they had to show for was proof of employment with their paychecks or tax records. One of the managers, Andrew "Rube" Foster (known as the father of black baseball) buckled under a tremendous amount of stress. Foster's health failed and he eventually went insane after a gas leak accident where he became deranged and was committed to an asylum in 1926.

Elston Howard who became the first "Black Yankee" for the New York Yankees eventually fell ill in 1979, but George Steinbrenner kept him on the payroll through 1980 when he returned worn out asking George for an executive office position. Elston was able to handle the job for a year, but didn't feel like his 'ole self. Much like Jackie Robinson, Elston faced unabated racism. Elston's wife and widow wrote a book about her husband and mentioned that her husband's life was cut short from the pressures and stress of coping with racism and the inability of climbing the administrative ladder to become a manager. Elston had taken the risk of standing by his own convictions and tried to succeed in spite of the powers and politics of the organization.

The Fair Employment Practices Act enacted by the New York State Legislature in 1945, followed the passing of the

Quinn-Ives Act banning discrimination in hiring. This gave Negro players and Negro employees a little more common legal ground in terms of employment. At the same time, Mayor Fiorello La Guardia formed the Mayor's Commission on Baseball to investigate integration of the major leagues. After the integration of the major leagues in 1947, as marked by the appearance of Jackie Robinson with the Brooklyn Dodgers, interest in Negro League baseball had waned. Although, some reports stated the New York Yankees were one of the last to accept integration in the major leagues.

Throughout the history of black baseball, teams struggled to find places to stay when we were traveling because we were not accepted in restaurants, motels/hotels and in most public places where the white people were. We usually entered through separate entrances, keeping us at a distance from the whites. In the early days, some of the teams would work at the hotels as staff employees by night, and play baseball games by day to entertain the guests, even though the hotels were segregated. We found these types of hotels were located mostly in New York and in Florida. Satchel, the team and I were no different and none of us were given any special treatment at these establishments. We were major league caliber-players, without the major league experience simply because of the color of our skin—but we could compete with the best of them. Public Broadcasting Atlanta interviewed me in 1993 where I stated, "That was the major leagues to the black community!"[33]

Major League Baseball started an "All-Star Game" in 1932. They started allowing fans to vote for their favorite players in 1947 in order to participate in a game between the National League and American League. The Negro Leagues also followed suit the same year, calling their game the "East-West" game. It was an annual All-Star game for the Negro League baseball players. This was an event that would showcase the best of the best players as well as put a spotlight on the league. It was THE dream and desire for every ballplayer to be an All-Star. On the flipside, it would be the owners' financial bonanza.

Each division's All-Star game was in Chicago. Comiskey Park was where the very first game was played on September 10th, 1933 before a large crowd of 20,000 people. As the Major Leagues moved their games to other cities, the Negro Leagues kept their games at Comiskey Park. The Negro League teams took advantage of the large black population in Chicago and fans were able to vote on the all-star players through black newspaper polls.

*Courtesy of Larry LeGrande. Photo of Larry
LeGrande in his catcher's uniform*

The Detroit Stars was a team in the Negro Leagues that played at Mack Park. Founded in 1919 in part by Rube Foster, owner and manager of the Chicago American Giants, the Detroit Stars established themselves as one of the most powerful teams in the West. After Mack Park burned down they moved to Hamtramck Stadium (known as Roesink Stadium today) in 1930 then to DeQuindre Park for their single season in the Negro American League.

Later in the season of 1958, Detroit Stars owner, Ted Rasberry renamed his team Goose Tatum's "Detroit Clowns" after Reece "Goose" Tatum, the clown prince of basketball's Harlem Globetrotters and a Negro League superstar. We also had other players on the team who were also famous basketball Globetrotters with the likes of Sherwood Brewer, Goose Tatum and Nathaniel "Sweetwater" Clifton. They spotlighted one of the great catchers, Bruce Petway who twice threw out Ty Cobb attempting to steal bases in a Cuban game. Then the team ended their operations in 1960.

In 1958, I joined the line-up of the Detroit Stars (Detroit Clowns) owner and fellow Negro League Baseball legend, Ted Raspberry. I was mostly a catcher, although sometimes played a little right field. The Kansas City Monarchs organization, also owned by Mr. Raspberry, Ted later brought me into town in 1959 where I caught for the legendary, Satchel Paige. I was a left-handed hitter, as well as a catcher and outfielder, which made me much more valuable on any team—finally *I Found Someone to Play With!*

Since that infamous day when I asked Ted Raspberry if I could play, he later sent me a letter to "come down and visit!" I made the team, but had trouble making the pitchers, so Ted was thinking of sending me to Grand Rapids, a minor negro league team. I had never seen pitchers quite this good, and just couldn't hit them. But I got adjusted in a hurry.

Enter, Ed "Stainless" Steele, a star in the Negro Leagues, playing in the Pacific Coast Leagues in Hollywood. Ed's average was between .320-.350. In spite of Ed's baseball spirit, Ed had a plate in his head and was beginning to fail which caused him to cut his career shorter than what he had planned. He told Ted, "to give me more time and to work with me, because I had all the tools". Ed saved me from going from Memphis to Grand Rapids. I saw fast-pitches and knee-breaking curveballs. As time passed on, I had forged tremendous throwing arm and I was moved to right field. That is when things really turned around for me because I was throwing runners out, trying to go from first to third on base hits, throwing runners out trying to tag up on fly balls, hit to right field attempting to score from third and was learning to catch these tremendous pitches.

Ed was my mentor and a good coach. While sitting in the dugout, I'd hear, "Larry move over to the right!" He could see the pitcher throwing and the balls were fouling to the right. He knew the batter couldn't pull the ball. He knew that he would hit the ball to me and sure enough, here comes the fly ball—right over to me! Ed was very good at analyzing the speed and the direction of the ball and could tell at what spot the ball would land and where it would be traveling. Piper Davis was also my mentor in helping me to learn how to hit the ball where it's pitched instead of trying to pull every pitch. I'm grateful to Piper who taught me the importance of fundamentals that we held in such high esteem.

On another occasion, we were slated to play the Memphis Red Sox in a town in Mississippi. There was no accommodations to change clothes for the game. No one would allow us to use their bathrooms in the area. We ended up finding a black-owned funeral parlor, and the owner was kind enough to let us in to use his facilities. There we were, in a large room with only a 40-watt bulb. The light was so dim, we could hardly find a spot to put our clothes down in this grim place as we changed into our uniforms. The smell was so strong that we rushed as fast as we could to change and get out of that gruesome place. Coincidentally, both teams had found this place to change, as there were no accommodations in the area. There were several caskets in the room. I draped my street clothes over one of the caskets as I was changing into my uniform. I tried not to look because it just so happened—there were bodies in the caskets. But, the game must go on! We all had to do, what we had to do!

Later on during the season, Satchel Paige joined the baseball team and they had the Clown Prince of Baseball—Reese "Goose" Tatum who also played throughout the world for royalty and presidential venues. Goose was doing basketball venues, exhibitions and other sports, but I insisted that he was a world-famous athlete, somewhat shy and did not like white people.

Ed Steele was one of the best managers I have ever had, because he invested in me and definitely saw my potential. I had to struggle to win the job because with five outfielders we had a top performing team. Ted wanted to send me to Grand Rapids, called the Grand Rapids Black Sox and Ed told him that, "We really need to keep Larry because we have a great baseball player here!" He saved me once again, from being sent to Grand Rapids. He played right field for the Birmingham Black Barons and Willie Mays was his teammate. Ed had a great throwing arm and I had eventually won him over with my strong throwing arm, and he was very pleased.

Ed just took me under his wing and taught me some things about being an outfielder. Birmingham had won the championship in the time that Ed played there. I went to Memphis as a catcher, and I was moved to right field—and that's where I was better suited. And when the Yankees signed me I was an outfield-catcher. I caught some games in the Winter league while I played outfield in the Winter League but in 1959, I really had to buckle down and finally won the job playing right field. This was my favorite position because that is where I could shine using my best throwing arm. When any base runner thought they could go from first to third on a base hit—I liked to challenge that. And after a few times of me shooting them down at third, *the word* and *respect* really got around.

I was playing catch with Satchel one day in foul territory. People were filing in and gazing at us and I am sure they wanted to get a good look at Satchel. One of my throws got away, and Satch had to reach way up high, way up almost out of his reach to get it. Satchel said to me, "Larry! Hey! What are you doing throwing way up there? There ain't nobody up there!" I remember people bursting out laughing when they heard him shouting that out.

Tommy LaSorda told me one day, "Hey, they just don't throw anymore!" We discussed that the game is not what it used to be. Good form is crucial to accuracy as well as appearance. We were proud to wear that uniform. We were clean cut and long hair was not allowed. Today, they have long hair like women, they're not clean shaven and dreadlocks along with slack in their pants. They don't have respect for the game of baseball or themselves. They just don't throw—you've got to throw to the bases. I've seen during the baseball exhibition, how many runners get thrown out—at the plate or going from first to third when the ball is in the outfield. They throw up the line over the catcher's head the majority of the time. When I had a routine fly ball coming in, I'd wait till the last second to gain the momentum after just standing there and studying where the ball was coming in. I feel that it was sloppy and disrespectful to the game of baseball.

Courtesy of Larry LeGrande. Photo of Larry LeGrande and Tommy LaSorda

I was quoted in a book entitled, ***"Black Barons of Birmingham: The South's Greatest Negro League Team and Its Players"***: "Larry LeGrande, a six-year veteran of the Negro Leagues, identified Jessie Mitchell as the second-best player he ever played against".[42] There was such camaraderie, pride and determination the Negro Leagues. While we played, we focused on our game. Jessie had played with the Monarchs as well as the Barons. I thought he was one of the best outfielders, but he also played with Satch and understood the fundamentals. I had played along with him in the All-Star games. He also mentioned that they don't play baseball like they used to and don't think about the fans—it's all about the money today and their fat checks. We played for the love of the game, but this sure doesn't exist today—we knew that the fans paid our salary back then. I knew Jesse was upset because he didn't make the majors because he certainly had the qualifications.

We would travel for three days straight only to get turned out at a local restaurant because the booking agents would book us in 300–400 mile jumps. You would pull your shoes off and put shower shoes on to take a shower. Then we'd try to put our shoes back on but we couldn't get them on because our feet were swollen. The booking agents didn't care how far apart, or for how long the trips would be or when they would book the teams—the bookings were what mattered. There was no planning and strategy to the bookings and we ended up all over the place. But, we loved to play baseball so we didn't mind much.

I recall giving a demonstration with my teammates to a little league team in Durham, North Carolina. There were about 100 kids there in a city park in 1958. We were playing the Monarchs at the time when I was with Detroit. You never saw such wide eyes in your life! We were in a city park because we were asked to come there instead of the Durham Bulls Ballpark. Ted Raspberry had sent us and the event turned out to be an exciting experience-for it was all black children. We taught them how to hold the bat, how to run the bases and how to field the catch the ball. We taught them the fundamentals.

Sam Thomas drove for the Memphis Red Sox, the team I played for in 1957. And "8" drove the Indianapolis Clowns when I played with them in 1958. These bus drivers would eat, sleep and fix the buses and literally lived in the bus for years. The drivers were paid pocket change and were not paid a salary and neither did the managers pay them. The players would pitch in and buy them food and beverages. We pledged to stand together in the face of ignorance and impoverishment.

Our workouts were a far cry from what baseball players do today. Our exercises consisted of your basic pushups, running in the outfield, and handgrips (all of us had handgrips) and or a rubber ball.

I remember the thing about playing on the Detroit Stars, is that they got more visibility from scouts and different teams because they played in more states. This is when the New York Yankees, the Minnesota Twins and Milwaukee Braves took interest in me. But I had always wanted to play for the New York Yankees because they beat the Dodgers most of the time, and Elston Howard played for New York with a .274 batting average because he had played for the Monarchs as well.

I continued to hit well and at the end of the 1958 season, I came home and wondered what was going to happen that year. I was beginning to wonder if I was ever going to get out of the Negro Leagues. Everyone was telling me that I played very well, I knew I was good and the newspapers continued to confirm my talent. I had found a purpose so big that it would challenge every fiber of my being to be at my best. In my self-discipline I knew that training was important because you can't win a game unless ***you're ready to win***.

I wanted to go play in a white man's league. I was really enjoying myself, but the Negro Leagues were not making any money and the rest of the players certainly didn't either.

I am still proud to this day, of my batting average for the Detroit Stars (later known as Detroit Clowns) at .318 in the Negro American League for that All-Star year in 1958.

As Detroit Stars season ended Satchel took a trip to Roanoke when "Goose" Tatum was playing basketball in the winter of 1958. Satchel appeared at "Goose" Tatum's game during half time to sign autographs and was introduced to the people that attended. Goose had his team and played first base in the Negro leagues.

I took Satchel and "Goose" back to my dad's house after the game. Satchel enjoyed being with my Dad, our guns and me, and we all loved to go hunting and fishing in the area. It was then that Satchel and I became close friends. Satchel loved to go fishing, hunting and target-practice and I was the only one from the teams that enjoyed the great outdoors as much as Satch did. Once in a while Goose would tag along when he had some free time.

I said to Satchel, "Hey Satch I can't wait for you to see the two huge bucks I took down along with my dogs—the dogs were running and running and I was able to take down two huge running bucks"! When I showed him the deer heads, Satchel turned to me and said, "Larry, the only way you could kill two huge bucks is if one had its head stuck up the other one's butt!" This was also Satch's way of telling me I was full of crap. The story was told a few times more on the bus with the team and we'd get laughs each and every time.

It was the year 1958, in baseball news, the headlines read in the World Series that the NY Yankees defeated the Milwaukee Braves 4 games to 3 in the best of seven series. I loved the Yankees and thought, ***one day, I'll be on their team.***

In the music and entertainment area, we were temporarily losing Elvis Presley to the United States Army and the radio waves were buzzing.

The Famous
Kansas City Monarchs

It would be the grandest surprise and experience of a lifetime to be the last catcher for one of the greatest pitchers of all time: Leroy Satchel Paige. I had felt a profound and absorbing interest in the man and his love for the game. He would change my life forever.

The longest running franchise in Negro League history was the Monarchs from Kansas City, Missouri. Originally owned by J. L. Wilkinson, a stern-looking, white business person who happened to own the most successful black team. Wilkinson sold the franchise after the 1948 season to Tom Baird, who continued to operate the Monarchs through most of the 1950s. By then it was a pseudo-minor league operation to the white Major Leagues and the team was then sold to Ted Raspberry. They attained ten pennants, tying the

Homestead Grays for the most flags by any Negro League team, and only one losing season in 1944, due to the fact that the team's roster was decimated by the loss of their players to the military during their stint with the Negro Leagues.

The Monarchs also had the distinction of having won the first World Series ever played between opposing leagues, in 1924 between the Negro National League and the Eastern League, and took the league's top honors winning the World Series again in 1942.

The Monarchs sent the most players into Major League Baseball after the color barrier was broken, of course. Some of the most notable players after Jackie Robinson, were Satchel Paige, Elston Howard, Ernie Banks, Hank Thompson and Willard "Home Run" Brown. This was the beginning of recognition and opportunity for some of the Negro players. Many of whom were just as good of athletes as the white players were.

During the days of the Great Depression, when the earlier Negro World Series played out, Leslie Wilkinson helped pioneer night baseball. The owner and creator of the Kansas City Monarchs would travel with their own spot lights. He installed a portable lighting system on the beds of trucks in 1930. The initial $50,000.00 system was so successful that it paid for itself during the team's spring training tour. The Great Depression hit black baseball much harder than the white Major Leagues.

The 1959 season started and spring training was in Birmingham with Satchel and "Goose" Tatum. Now I had become a seasoned baseball player. I could catch, throw, run the bases, and hit with the best. I was a natural player, a .300-plus hitter because I learned to hit the ball to all fields. We played in Washington D.C. the home of the Washington Senators at Griffith Stadium with 32,000 people in attendance.

During that time, we had one manager and he called the shots. The manager in these instances was manager *and* coach. Ted Raspberry was the business manager/owner. But, Frank Evans was all three: manager, coach and player. Frank turned out to be one of my co-players. Just prior to my career in baseball, Frank had already played on the teams that I had played with as well as others. Frank and I were discussing this particular game when he playing for the Cleveland Buckeyes in Yankee Stadium against the Black Yankees once had 70,000 people in attendance, which were impressive numbers back then. When the game was over, the Buckeyes got $3,000.00 the Black Yankees got $3,000.00. The players would get very disturbed by this because we knew the price of the tickets; those tickets were $1.00 each. This happened more often than not because as the Negro Leagues had started to fold, there weren't many teams left and contracts were not established at this point either. They played local teams and their East-West games. There were six teams left at this point: Monarchs, Barons, Detroit Stars, Raleigh Tigers, Memphis Red Sox, and New Orleans Bears. The Bears and the Tigers were not considered Negro Teams, but they were in the League. Many of the players had begun barnstorming to make extra money.

I recall one of the insurmountable problems that we encountered in our games was the every-day corruption. One of the games drew 32,000 fans. We could see AND count the people in the stands, but we only got paid for 16,000. Where did the 50 percent of the income go? It's anyone's guess as to what happened there. What were we to do when no one was on our side? The promoters and bookies were taking a large share of the money at the time. Another example was that we had 65,000 fans in attendance for the Cleveland Buckeyes and the NY Black Yankees. They each got $9,000.00. The tickets were $1.50, so where did the remainder of the income go once again? We would stare with blinders on from the dugout at the tens of thousands of fans. We were the attraction and we should have been paid more. We didn't understand all the inner-workings of expenses to run teams around the countryside. Ted Raspberry was an extremely wealthy man—more than all of us put together. We thought Ted should give up a little bit more of his take.

Our annual contract showed that we were paid $200.00 a week, after we paid taxes and social security our take home was about $170.00. The players' and managers' income was always under scrutiny—with the owners, each and every year. So, if we played 10 games a month, Ted Raspberry would take in at least $80,000.00 with an average of 20 players on our team, and payroll would be about $16,000.00

The scrutiny and negotiations would come into play every year, when the owners would put pressure on the players for their performance from the prior year. It was an annual battle year after year. We needed to perform better and better each year, or they would cut our pay. They would justify their negotiations because maybe our stats were less than what they wanted, or if we were hurt in a game and the performance diminished. But if our stats were good, the negotiations would be on the other foot to increase our pay. We had to be our own agents to negotiate the contracts, but we weren't agents. Many of us did have formal education or had only made it through high school. If the owner had knowledge that the players had a shady or questionable background, they held it over their heads in negotiations; these particular players would settle for less.

Appealing to the urgent temper of youth, sometimes events took an unexpected sinister turn. I only had one altercation however, with one ballplayer originally from Philadelphia that envied me for some time. The team was getting on the bus, finding their seats and putting their stuff down. I was about to sit down in my seat and he firmly tapped me on my shoulder, I turned, and ***he punched me in the nose!*** He was so jealous of my talent and my baseball career. He had hit me for no reason at all. I tried to return the punch and then I heard, "Break it up!". I was looking for a bat on the bus just to hit him. I felt like killing him, but I knew that my career would be over with. He thought he was being cut from the team and just sucker-punched me. Ted Raspberry soon after that intolerable incident, released him from the team, and a few years later I learned that he had passed away.

On a clear, hot summer's afternoon, in 1959 we played in Lima's Industry Park in Ohio against the Metros. We won 7–1 and collected nine hits in front of almost 1,000 fans. I was playing right field with five at bats, one RBI, one homer. *The Lima News* wrote, "Kansas City snipped the knot in the fifth as Larry LeGrande led off with a solo homer. He tagged the first pitch, parking it out of sight over the left field fence." It was an exciting game for all of us as the article went on to say, "The Monarchs padded it another tally in the ninth as Bill Davis hit a three-bagger off a light pole in right and manager, Sherwood Brewer skied out to deep center sacrificing Davis home. Both clubs had came up with a double play. The Metros went around the horn for theirs, from Ron Foltz at third to Ron Bonanno at second to Bill Guice at first. Kansas City's Washington stabbed a line drive and doubled a runner off of first in the eighth on a superb throw for the Monarch twin-killing throw."[15]

Tuscaloosa, Alabama was the next stop for the Monarchs. The coach told me to warm up another pitcher, yet again, but it was my day of rest. The next thing I knew, the coach called me in to pinch hit. This time, it was worse than stage fright. This unexplained anxiety hit me one more time. There were thousands of eyes glaring at me. The fans and my teammates were yelling out my name. It was a crucial time in the game, and the first pitch was a strike one fastball—I was struck with downright fear—it was intimidating. ***It was like a bullet, I almost got killed!*** The breakneck speed of the ball sounded like a firecracker exploding two feet behind me as it pounded the catcher's mitt. It was another hot summer's day, and there I was, a standing frozen icicle. The second pitch was a curve ball in for strike two, and a change up for strike three. I never took the bat off my shoulder. When I finally returned to the dugout, I heard the blast from the coach, "What the hell are you doin'!?" I couldn't even answer him. I thought to myself, that was one talented pitcher! My year with the Monarchs was busy, we visited thirty-three states which was more than enough for any teenager to handle, big boys or not.

In 1959, I played a game at Yankee Stadium with Willie Washington, Satchel called him "Josh." He hit one that never got more than twenty feet off the ground to direct center field and over the monuments. The monuments were 461 feet away and the 30,000 fans in attendance were stunned in a jaw-dropping moment—seldom seen before—if ever. It sounded like a shotgun going off as it hit and then continued to bounce around.

I always thought Roberto Clemente had the best throwing arm ever. I like Carl Furillo very much, too. Dave Parker was good, with a good, strong arm, but I thought he always threw a little high. Had I made it to the pros, I believe my strong and accurate throwing arm would have ranked right behind Furillo.

My other favorites were Willie Mays, Ted Williams and Mickey Mantle and Willie Washington, and my teammate in the AAA team, who we called "Wash". Willie hit eight home runs in four games. It was a shame, because he was only in his thirties. He hit the ball in Yankee Stadium past the monument; he hit the ball in Saginaw over the stadium and in Winnipeg wop-sided the ball out of the stadium. He played third base and loved it. It is good to have a good throwing arm but it is most important to have accuracy. I'm grateful for the friendship I had with Willie Mays as many people said I was a lot like him on the field.

In thinking about my decisions over the past few years in the leagues, I had four teams that wanted to sign me. My regret is that I should have gone to the Braves because I loved Hank Aaron. It would have been an honor to play with him, but then again, I would have never ended up on Satch's All-Star team. Thinking about what it was, I recall Satchel saying to me one day, "Don't try to think!" You're going to get everybody in trouble—thinking is a hard job".

We traveled over to Muscatine, Iowa in June of 1961 to play at the Tom Bruner Field. The Red Sox was splitting a double-header with the Rock Island Nationals and the Kansas City Monarchs. Satch, Ira and I were among the Monarchs eager to play the Red Sox for some time. I was playing right field, and my friend Ira was playing center—course Satch was pitching for us. *The Muscatine Journal and News Tribune* wrote, "Paige, who receives top billing with the traveling Monarchs worked the first two innings for the visitors. He walked John Robinson, the second man to face him, and was tagged for a single down the right field line by Don Calvert; who was thrown out at second trying to stretch hit into a double.

Satch, the ageless pitching wonder, fanned two in demonstrating a fairly quick fastball and a tantalizing change-up which a couple of local boys popped up. Jim White relieved Paige in the third and finished up the duel of three-hitters with McCleary. Both of Kansas City's two unearned markers came in on the fifth. McCleary had retired one man when first baseman John Winston's fly ball to right was dropped by Calvert. Winston then stole second and went to third when catcher Don Grensing's throw landed in center field. He scored on Johnny Walker's single. Another single this time by leadoff man Larry LeGrande, produced the second run after Walker took second on an in-field out and advanced to third on a wild pitch. The only other hit off McCleary was a first inning single. A walk to Calvert, infield out and Bob Herr's two-out double gave the Sox their only run in the bottom of the fifth. John Robinson's long fly-ball ended the threat."[24]

We won over the Red Sox 2–1 in that game. I had three at bat, no runs, one hit and one RBI. Satch had one at bat. Johnny had the other RBI that nailed the game. I guess Don hadn't gotten the word about my strong accurate arm, 'cus I gunned him down at second.

We had arrived in Iola, Kansas in August of 1961. I was playing along with Ira McNight, Washington and Satch against the Detroit Stars. I played second base this time, Ira was catching and Satch pitched a perfect inning giving up no runs and no hits. *The Iola Register* stated, "There was more hitting and scoring than there was in the last Monarch game here. The Monarchs had 11 hits, Detroit 12. Both left base runners every inning but one". Ira hit a homer with one out for us and the Monarchs were thrilled. The newspaper went on to say, "Trailing 5–1 in the ninth, the Stars scored two runs on two singles, two walks and a fielder's choice. That left two out with our Washington up after a batter was hit to fill the runways." Although, we lost this game 7–5, everyone thought it was a worthwhile endeavor for the Jaycees' Junior Baseball Program."[23]

In August of 1961, we drove to Wellsville, New York to play the Detroit Stars. By this time, we'd captured the league title twenty-five times and I was billed as the "Monarch Star". *The Wellsville Daily Reporter* announced, "Look for a large turnout tonight when the World's Champion Kansas City Monarchs appear at Tullar Field to meet the Detroit Stars in an official Negro American League contest." Willie Washington was going to announce his starting pitcher with the Stars just before game time. They printed a full photo of me with my bat, beneath the photo read, "Larry LeGrande, a 5'10" 19-year old outfielder will be in the Kansas City Monarchs lineup tonight at Tullar Field. LeGrande has a good throwing arm and is a better than average base runner. He hails from Roanoke, Virginia." Although they said I was nineteen at the time, I had just turned twenty-two years old. They also mentioned that Ted Raspberry stated that five of us were slated for the major leagues two of which, myself and Ike Brown billed for the Tigers.[25]

We returned to Hays, Kansas in mid-July of 1962 to play Goose Tatum's Harlem Stars. *The Hays Daily News* reported, "A large turnout is expected Thursday night when the world's champion Kansas City Monarchs appear at the Hays Ballpark against Goose Tatum's Harlem Stars." They went on to say that the Kansas City team "is the most popular traveling outfit to appear in the mid-west and is loaded youngsters who will definitely see action in some major league organization in the near future. Monarch's owner Ted Raspberry says four of his players—Ira McNight, Larry LeGrande, Roger Brown and George Davis—are billed for the major leagues next season. Davis is pegged for the Cleveland Indians; McNight to the New York Yankees; and LeGrande and Brown to the Detroit Tigers."[21]

I had played a season from 1957–1958 with each of the Memphis Red Sox, Detroit Stars (Detroit Clowns) and the Kansas City Monarchs (1959–1961) leading the Negro Leagues in out field assists all three seasons, bar none, as well as batting a .334. The Monarchs were not just any team—they were billed as the World Champion Kansas City Monarchs. I was in the famous Negro League that had propelled Jackie Robinson on his path to the Brooklyn Dodgers and the breakthrough against the big league color line. I was proud to be among them. It was truly a tremendous feets of athleticism and focus when Jackie Robinson was playing. He would play under tremendous pressure of people yelling, screaming and cussing at him. He had to block everything out with the most concentration we've ever seen and still hit the ball the way he did.

The Management—
Make Or Break

The first manager that I had was Homer "Goose" Curry who helped me get to the Negro Leagues in Memphis in 1957. The second year with the Detroit Stars was where I really dug my heels in and learned the game of baseball. This is where I met Ed Steele, who managed the Detroit Stars. I was paid $200.00 a month with Ted Raspberry. Ed played right field on the Birmingham Black Barons and on this team were Willie Mays and Piper Davis, also the manager of the Barons. Ed had played AAA Baseball in Oakland, the Texas League and the Pacific Coast League, and in his last year was with Fort Worth at fifty-four years old. In 1959, there was Sherwood Brewer along with Ernie Banks who formed the Double Play Combination with the Kansas City Monarchs. I'm grateful for Sherwood who took me under his wing to show me some of his fundamentals of baseball. This is the same man who also directed Jackie Robinson and Ernie Banks on infield techniques prior to their embarking in the major leagues.

I had a lot of respect and admiration for Ernie Banks, as Ernie would come by the players' hotel to visit, talk with the players and watch them play. I distinctly remember a time when I was still in high school and my parents insisted that I work in the garden before listening to the radio and hearing Ernie Banks playing for the Monarchs. I later recounted to Ernie when I met him about the times I was listening about him over the radio and then finally becoming pro player, which made him smile ear to ear. Ernie left the Kansas City Monarchs and went straight to the Chicago Cubs, although I think he was hesitant and maybe even reluctant to go. He was a fine, classy example of how the Negro Leaguers played in competition in both the Negro Leagues and the Major Leagues.

In 1958, I played in Comiskey Park—the home of the Chicago White Sox. Enter, Jackie Robinson, in the dugout dressed up in his beautiful brown suit. Jackie said, "Hey, Ernie, I never hear from you guys". Ernie replied, "Hey, we never hear from you!" Ernie introduced Jackie to the team. I do remember like it was yesterday, that Jackie had the firmest, hardest handshake—like he meant it. It was a real thrill for me to shake hands with one of the great and most important sports figures in history.

Satchel had stayed at the Street Hotel at 18th Street and the Paseo. This was a lodging and entertainment establishment for blacks since the early 1900's. The Street Hotel was home to the Blue Room that staged famous and legendary jazz shows with famous entertainers. The hotel had a top-notch national reputation for housing entertainers, sports icons and numerous movie stars. The Street Hotel was owned and operated by Mr. Reuben Street from 1919 until his passing in 1956. Situated at 1508–1512 East 18th Street in the 18th and Vine district, for many years it was the sultry, smokey and extravagant go-to place in the region for entertainment, relaxation, socializing and hob-nobbing with some interesting and famous people. The hotel was made up of fifty rooms, the exclusive entertainment club Blue Room, the Rose Room restaurant, beauty and barber shops as well as a pharmacy; it was well ahead of its time. Many famous people stayed at Street's, and some played pool next door at Jones billiards, including famous likes of Count Basie, Joe Louis, and Duke Ellington. Others who stayed at the famous hotel were Jackie Robinson, Ella Fitzgerald, Cab Calloway, Dinah Washington, Lionel Hampton, the Harlem Globetrotters and of course, Satchel Paige and myself.

The streets were packed at night with people walking, shopping and listening to music floating through the air from the speakeasies and restaurants. We could smell all kinds of aromas coming from restaurants as we would walk by. We absorbed the perfumes and colognes that people would douse themselves with because they were always dressed-to-kill, especially for the night life. Because this was mostly a black people's hotel we would congregate there and the Monarchs would play day and night games. If there were no games, we'd pass the time in the hotel because there was so much to do and see and the area reminded me a lot like today's Las Vegas.

Many times we would run into the entertainers and talk about how sometimes they wished they were baseball players instead of musicians and then we would tell them we wished sometimes we were musicians. Many times we would see them attend the ballgames at the park or come out to swing a bat. We'd also enter the speakeasies and some of the greats would be there and they'd show us how to play the saxophone or piano. I guess that happens in many walks of life and to many of us where we dream of being in someone else's shoes.

The American Jazz Museum today, also located in the 18th Street area, touts old time pictorials and stories of the area and speakeasies in the 1930s and later into the 1940s. They claim the Blue Room as one of the hottest nightspots in the region yielding the excitement of the evolution of jazz as this type of music is what brought everyone together for enjoyment and relaxation. Today, that legacy plays on as part of the American Jazz Museum as many of the jazz figures came up from the Deep South such as New Orleans-style of music and entertainment. The region was the basis for black economic growth and development including black education, social gatherings and established organizations. "The Bowery" was also home to thousands of black residents at the turn of the century whereby they would gather and enjoy an evening out, with food and entertainment.

The *Kansas City Star* wrote: "the first true organization opened for business in 1920, when the Negro National League formed from meetings at the Street Hotel and the Paseo YMCA in Kansas City. The Kansas City Monarchs joined the American Giants of Chicago, the ABCs of Indianapolis, the St. Louis Stars and a team of traveling Cubans, the Western Cuban All-Stars in the league. The Eastern Colored league was formed in 1923 with teams in Brooklyn, New York, Baltimore, Hillsdale (a Philadelphia suburb) and the Eastern Cuban All-Stars. Four world series took place from 1924–27 and seven more in the 1940s. The Monarchs captured the first flag, and their 62–17 record of 1929 was a Negro League record."[40]

This beautiful Early-American region had sidewalks filled with entertainers, baseball players and jazz artists. Reaching over them were one to two-story buildings with Italianate and Queen Anne detailing. Many of the buildings were small businesses where the proprietors resided above their stores. Yet, another important building that stood proud with beautiful terra cotta facade was the Star Theatre, later renamed the Gem Theatre which housed vaudeville entertainers and motion pictures for the black community. Imagine strolling down the street and hearing jazz music and many forms of New Orleans style music wherever you walked.

Although blacks had their own community, outside of our community we were allowed to buy most products in most stores. However, we were restricted in some instances in receiving credit or trying on clothes in the white half of society. We just weren't there yet.

During the 1920's and 1930's the Kansas City Monarchs were the most famous black baseball team in the country. Their offices were also located in the popular 18th and Vine District. This area was popular in terms of business, music, pool halls and theaters. The Monarchs later relocated to the Lincoln Building by 1940 housing other elite organizations for black commercial business. Parades were held in the main streets each year to mark opening day for the Monarchs celebrating the team and their fantastic accomplishments. Having those parades honored the individuals, and the townspeople were so very proud. As store owners, business people, families and ministers supported the team—they were viewed as very good role models. They brought national attention to the city, extensive commerce and a lot of prestige throughout their athletic accomplishments, namely the famous baseball athletes such as Satchel Paige and Jackie Robinson.

Soon after the 1960s the Vine District fell into decline as famous musicians and stars looked for additional fame and fortune in the big cities such as New York, Los Angeles, Hollywood and Chicago.

The Negro Leagues Baseball Museum is situated in the famous Vine District displaying and honoring some of the history, life, culture of the area and many of the baseball players of its heyday. I feel that without the women, the Negro Leagues would have been dead. They were somewhat like the first cheerleaders on the sidelines. No sport is played without the women. They were our enjoyment and our stress-relievers. Nevertheless, they did get us in more trouble than what it was worth. However, when we were on the bus, talking about the women we met from the previous stop or game, it was always a topic of discussion on the bus and most entertaining for the team.

Jackie Robinson was one of the people who meant a great deal to me. I met him twice, once in Chicago and again in Kansas City. He loved the game, and as famous as he was, he did not know what ego was. It was such an achievement to be a Monarch, for a black player. In the Monarchs thirty-year tenure won ten Negro League pennants and two Negro League World Series. They were the longest running team in the league and closed shop in 1965.

Even though the Monarchs had gained national attention, sitting at a Monarchs game you would see and experience segregation. The whites would sit any where they pleased in the best seats. There was no assigned seating back then. But at a Blues game, (NY Yankees' top minor league affiliate), they made the blacks sit in the right-field bleachers beyond a chicken-wire fence. The ugly face of segregation always appeared and made us feel like we were the chickens being fenced in—or fenced out in this case.

I remember the era when Jackie broke the 'color barrier'. All of the Negro players were absolutely overwhelmed with excitement and at the same time feelings of trepidation when this happened. This was a major headline in all the newspapers and everyone was talking about it. When Jackie came to Brooklyn to play, a black man was sitting in front of this white man and when Jackie came to the plate, the black man stood up and clapped. The white man sitting behind him took a stick and split his head open. Some people standing nearby put a rag on the gash and carried the black man out. Nothing happened to the white man and of course he wasn't arrested. The game continued on in spite of what happened.

Satchel told me about a terrifying event was in the form of a letter to Jackie, it was from the Ku Klux Klan: "Nigger-boy Robinson, if you play in tonight's game against the Cincinnati Reds, you will be killed". Sometimes Satch or Jackie would see threatening graffiti on the walls telling them not to play or they would die. 'Pee Wee' Reese also gave the Negro players an olive branch from the Dodgers as he played alongside Robinson. Reese, an All-Star player out of nearby Kentucky had seen the terrifying actions as a boy and what his father had shown him growing up with the KKK lynchings.

Cincinnati fans were screaming, cussing and yelling threats at Robinson. It was an incredibly tough time as the Dodgers took the field in the bottom of the first. In a show of support, Reese who was playing short stop, temporarily left his position and traveled over to Robinson at first base and put his arm around the rookie. You could hear a pin drop in this show of racial empathy by Reese.

Satchel told me stories about an absolute racist baseball commissioner, named Kenesaw Mountain Landis. He was the first baseball commissioner during his twenty-five year tenure who blocked most attempts to integrate the game.

It was well known that he delayed actions to integrate the baseball leagues. Satchel was still at the top of his game, striking out and averaging fifteen strikeouts a day, and Landis, counted this as a detriment. He mentioned that Joe DiMaggio was the only one that could hit against Satchel.

Satch had told me one day, "Larry, save everything you can about us, 'cus they won't believe it anyhow, 'cus, I'm so much older than you." I promised that I would, and now that I've collected our story, I decided to share this with the world as I turn seventy-six years of age.

In The Field of Dreams with
New York Yankees

Near the end of the 1959 season, my manager called me over during batting practice. Before the game started, Ted motioned to me to come out of the dugout. Ted tells me to "come upstairs"; feeling a little unnerved by all this, I was escorted by the ushers and ended up in one of the immense conference rooms. I laughed to myself because I had never seen carpet flowing all the way up the walls, plush and opulent—for the owners and executives to have their outrageous meetings, luncheons and discussions of how to move players around like pawns on a chessboard. There in the plush, magnificent large offices overlooked the field at Washington's Griffith Stadium, with carpet so thick it threw you off-balance. In the room were two big league scouts with big diamond rings and gold necklaces. Ted said, "Larry, have a seat." They asked me how I was doing, and I said, "I'm fine", very nervously. They were introduced to me as "the men who were scouts for the New York Yankees". They proceeded to tell me, "We're here to sign you to the Yankees." I said, "What!? How could that be?" They asked and pummeled me with more questions, and quickly asked me to sign a contract. Then they asked me, "What was your proudest moment"? Without hesitation I said, "Signing this contract!" *I inked my name on a Yankees contract!*

However, later on, I found out that it truly was not the proudest moment of my baseball career. As 1959 rolled on, Satchel, Goose and I continued to play with the Monarchs until season's end. At which time, I reported to the Yankee's Winter League in St. Petersburg.

The NY Yankees Minor League Director, Johnny Johnson called me when the 1959 Monarch's season ended. He asked me if I objected to flying to Tampa. I did not know, because I had never flown before. I headed to the airport and ended up in Tampa as requested. I was not used to being serviced by ushers either. During Negro League era, you carry your own luggage, clean your own uniforms and shine your own shoes. I was treated like a celebrity; they took me in a limousine, carried my luggage and took me over the thirteen-mile long Tampa Bay Bridge to St. Petersburg at the Laura Lee Hotel that was for players in winter baseball. *I thought I had died and gone to heaven.* The next let down? The driver dropped me at a seedy hotel, that was only for the black players on the 'colored' side of town and whisked the white teammates off to a comfortable, attractive hotel across town.

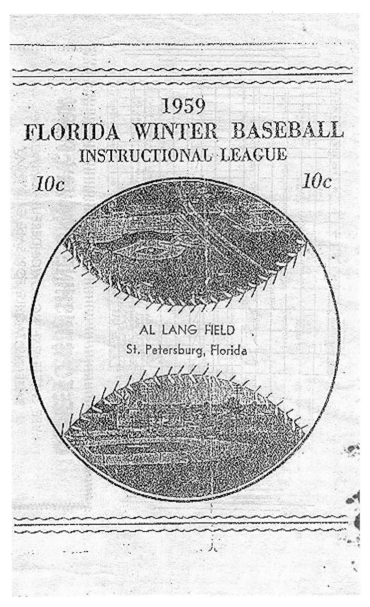

Courtesy of Larry LeGrande. 1959 Florida Winter Baseball. Part 1
Instructional League Program. Al Lang Field, St. Petersburg, Florida

Courtesy of Larry LeGrande. 1959 Florida Winter Baseball. Instructional League Program Part 2. Al Lang Field, St. Petersburg, Florida

I played in the Winter Leagues with the New York Yankees, and had to cope with the hostilities thrown in front of me. I stayed at the Laura-Lee hotel in St. Petersburg, Florida during spring training and I had never been on a team of all white folks. It was a hell of a transition from all black to all white players. I could hear the juke box from the nightclub next door sending blues music through the air from the famous B.B. King, Muddy Waters and Elmore James until 2:30 a.m. every night. I was staying with Dave Ricketts and Johnnie Lewis who played for the Cardinals. After the music stopped, my roommates would start 'rattling us all night long'. Johnnie Lewis asked me one morning as we headed to the field, "Hey, Larry, you've been yawning for a couple of hours, are you getting enough sleep?" I said, "Yes, I am," but Johnnie knew the answer was really "No." In spite of some of these sleepless nights, I stayed on top of my game.

In 1959, we closed out our Winter League season schedule at Al Lang Field against Cleveland's minor league team winning 4–2. I was playing right field and we (Saints/ Yankees Minor League), had 7 hits combined. The *St. Petersburg Times* wrote, "The Yankees collected seven hits with Jim Horton and Joe Pepitone each getting two singles, Oscar Pickering, Larry LeGrande, and Bud Zipfel had the other three."[10]

THIS IS THE "SPRING" IN SPRING TRAINING: St. Petersburg Saints candidates Julian Vicente, on ground, and Larry LaGrand, go through their paces up at Woodlawn Park while some of the squad watches. Julian is out of the Dominican Republic, and LaGrand hails from Roanoke, Va.
(Independent photo by Charlie Mohn)

Reprinted with permission. Tampa Bay Times. Larry LeGrande, St. Petersburg Saints Spring Training.

I was with the Saints playing the New Yankees minor league in April of 1960 when we played the Tampa Tarpons. We had kicked off the Florida State League with this game in early spring. Although we lost in a close game 8–7, *The Evening Independent* stated, "LE GRANDE SLUGS. Larry LeGrande, Saint right-fielder, was the big gun of the afternoon for the locals. He punched a single and lashed a triple in three tries."[26]

As spring training ended, I knew I had to find an alternative sleeping situation to stay competitive on the ballfield. Because of all the cussing, loud noises and music from the nightclub next door and all that damned snoring I really wasn't getting enough sleep.

There was a black man standing in front of the Laura-Lee Hotel. I stopped to chat with him and told him of my dilemma and asked him if he knew of some place that I could stay. He said, "I know of a place. Walk straight up 3rd Avenue, several blocks up." As he pointed to the house. I went right up to the house, rang the doorbell and asked the woman who opened the door if she had a room to rent for the baseball season. She gave me a room for $30.00 a month. Yet, another chance meeting on the sidewalk!

As the season started, I ended up moving into that private home with a black school teacher. During the segregation era and every year at spring training in St. Petersburg, the Cardinal's black players stayed at the Laura-Lee as the Cardinals also had their spring training facility in St. Petersburg. When the black players returned for their regular home games season they sought out private black residences in many cases.

If I used her kitchen, on occasion, I would give her extra money. I ended up having bad feelings about her though. I gave her a tip one day, just out of the kindness of my heart and out of the blue. The next thing I knew, she raised the rent! When she perceived how much money I was making. I just put up with it, because I didn't want to go back to the loud racket from the Laura Lee Hotel. Although she was a black woman, she opened her door to me in my time of need, but opportunistic greed knows no color.

I would read the New York papers, when I could get a copy, just to keep up with the New York Yankees as I stayed in hotels and waited for our the next game. It would feed my dream to some day put on the pin stripes.

I heard some of my teammates saying racial comments within listening distance and sometimes they would say these horrible things to my face as well. The whites disrespected me every moment. But when they saw I could play, *things changed dramatically.*

It took me over a week to gain the white team's respect, when they saw me throwing the ball from the outfield at about three feet from the ground. Of course, today I am suffering with rotator-cuff problems in my shoulder, but I would not trade it for the world.

I had to prove myself in the minors. I was stepping into a baseball field that was very contentious. Curtis Johnson was another who had to prove himself as well.

One day, as we were traveling with the team we stopped at a restaurant. We were in two station wagons with St. Petersburg Saints painted on the sides. The team proceeded to go in to eat. And of course, I had to stay behind in the car, as they didn't allow blacks in this particular restaurant. Eventually, the team manager's afterthought was to send the waitress out to take my order. I ordered a couple of hamburgers and a strawberry milkshake. As the players finished their meal and returned to the cars, I asked the waitress to bring me another hamburger to-go. The team manager said to her, "Go get him his order!" She replied, "Why don't you go get it! I want to stay here and talk to him!" But he didn't give her the chance and he sent her off to get my order.

Despite the segregation issues and the early treatment by my teammates, this was one of the most enjoyable leagues that I played in. There was no hustle and bustle like the Negro Leagues. When we hit town, in the Negro Leagues, the first stop was usually the laundry mat. We had to wash all of our own uniforms and jock straps in preparation of each game. With the St. Petersburg Saints, I simply walked in the locker room and my uniform was hanging, pressed and cleaned, and my shoes were shined. I got dressed and went to play ball. The anticipation of playing with Elston Howard (who played with Jackie Robinson and played on the Kansas City Monarchs) was just overwhelming. I was one step away from the major leagues.

I was hitting .304 leading the Florida State League third for the League in triples, third for the League in runs batted in and got released. When I tell players today black or white, what I had led the league in, and still got released, they would say, "That is a damned shame! That sounds like the old racist Yankees!" These days, some players get called up to the major leagues hitting only .240.

The fans were in their best when they were jovial and were looking forward to that big game. The fans really liked me and were great. I happened to be the only black person on this baseball team. It was very strange for me at twenty years of age to have only played in the Negro Leagues with all blacks to transition to a team with all white players.

My teammates would show their resentment and anger when a black player got a hit for the opposing team. My team would shout, "Dammit the dumb black ass got a hit!" Then, they'd remember that I was sitting in the dugout and cover their mouth with embarrassment and turn away from me because they'd forget I was even there.

The Line Up card was distributed at 10 cents a piece in 1959 as people would line up to see us and ask for our autographs. We were used to having people coming up to us for our autographs, whether it was on the street, at the park, or following us to our hotel. Most of the time, most of them were women.

The white players stayed several miles from the training facility while I was the only one staying in a local hotel that was for blacks only. I don't know exactly where the white players stayed, but it was about five miles away—I didn't give a damn where they stayed. We never socialized after game times—the only friends I made were made in the streets. Eventually the management forced integration in baseball from where we stayed in hotels, ate in restaurants, rode in the buses and public transportation, but it would be very slow to come around.

The next morning, I was brought to the Miller Huggins field (named for the Yankees manager). I was thinking to myself: *I'm a Yankee now. A New York Yankee.*

This is where I met Jerry Coleman a great second baseman that played for the NY Yankees; Joe Pepitone who played for the New York Yankees and Chicago Cubs; Clete Boyer both of which showed no signs of racism toward me. Bill Stafford who hit for the Yankees; Ed Lopat, who played for the Chicago White Sox and New York Yankees then traded to Baltimore Orioles; Ernest Johnson who also played for the Monarchs. I was starting at the bottom in minor league ball, but this was the Yankees organization. Some teammates gave the cold shoulder and didn't talk to me unless they had to. ***But I had a dream.*** And within the first month of the season, I led the team in runs batted in. Led the Florida State League in triples. The local sports writer titled me as the best outfielder there was.

Two weeks after I signed, we played a triple header National Park Stadium in Washington, D.C. There were 32,000 people there on a Sunday morning *I had signed with the Yankees*. It was a long bus ride, but I was primed for the day. We played in Baltimore at a racetrack and by Sunday evening, we were playing in Philadelphia. We just kept our uniforms on. It was summertime, and we pushed the windows down because it didn't smell too good on the bus.

I had started playing with mostly all black but by the end of the season, it was mostly all whites. It still wasn't easy.

First thing we did was shake hands and start warming up in the field. On December 27th, 1959 was when training started. I had what they called a Class B Contract and then received an assignment to Greensboro in North Carolina. Finally, a few days later, I got a phone call saying "not to report" (to Greensboro, NC) that I would be stationed in St. Pete, Florida because "there was some black people that boycotted the lunch counter in Greensboro"—and I certainly didn't want to get caught up in the racist conflict that was going on over there. So, I did not get to play in the Carolinas. The Greensboro "Sit Ins" was a series of non-violent protests leading to increased national sentiment over segregation at a crucial period in our United States history. Originally, the primary event took place at the Greensboro, North Carolina Woolworth's store, which is now the International Civil Rights Center and Museum. Even though it was not the first of the protests that took place in 1960, this led to the Woolworth's department store chain reversing its policy on racial segregation.

Later in the 1959 season, with Kansas City Monarchs, I was called to play for the Yankees in the Florida State Minor League. I was released later after spring training in 1960 and returned to the Kansas City Monarchs.

I had signed with the New York Yankees in 1959 and led the Class A Florida State League with the St. Petersburg Saints in 1960 with a .304 average, third in the league in triples, third in the league in runs scored and RBIs. In my first 30 games, I started hot. I batted in 12 runs and scored 11 more in my first 57 at bats.

I really didn't know the racism ran so deeply, especially in the south. I became very bitter about the situation, but I tried for quite some time to get it through my mind that it was life and I just had to move on.

The Sunday Independent, wrote "Just in time the St. Petersburg Saints have found the formula—they're winning baseball games (just clicking off five in a row). And they face a two-day home meeting with the front running Sanford Greyhounds." They went on to say, "The Saints picked up a couple of unearned runs in the second and fourth innings Friday night to take a 2–1 margin into the late frames. In the ninth, Larry LaGrande and Paul Dolinsky walked. LaGrande romped home on Julian Vincente's single. The final was 3–1." I was playing right-fielder that day, with three at bats, 2 runs and one hit. The article went on to say, "A sweep of the Saturday and Sunday Lang Field series and manager Stan Charnofsky has his young'uns roosting on the top. The Saints have won 10 and dropped six."[38]

In another game against Orlando, we ended a 3–1 victory, Julio Anglanda was a young hurler from the Dominican Republic with an impressive arm. *The St. Petersburg Times,* wrote "Tonight the red hot Saints return to the friendly surrounding of Al Lang field for a two-game home stand with first place Sanford. A St. Petersburg sweep could push the Saints to the top of the FSL heap." The standings reported the Saints average as .625, Vincente's average was number one on the team with a .333 batting average and I followed second with a .323, Stan was right behind me with a .314.[39]

Stan Charnofsky was my manager when I was playing in St. Petersburg. He was also a good player on our team and played in the minor leagues until 1966. Stan was put into political positions more than once during his tenure with the St. Petersburg Saints. On this occasion, he had the dubious honor of releasing me. Stan had received THE call from

Johnny Johnson to release me. Stan called me into his office. As I walked in, I'd never seen a man's eyes so full of fear, not knowing if I was going to explode and how I was going to handle this news. Stan told me, "The Yankees released you". I stood paralyzed and speechless. My dignity counseled me to be silent. He went on to say, "I don't understand it myself, they said, 'they wouldn't pay the remainder of the contract to the Monarchs'." As I stood in shock, Stan went on to say, "The only reason I think you were cut was racial-bias." Although Stan couldn't relay this reason in the public eye, he knew he'd be fired as well. I simply turned and walked out of his office. Went to take a shower in the locker room, then left and walked ten blocks to my boarding house from Al Lang Field. I felt like jumping into Tampa Bay. My constraint was excruciating. All I could do was re-play my hitting, my strong throwing arm, my base running, all my hits and home runs. How could this happen?

The following day, Herb Smith the team's owner and Mitchell Mick, team secretary told me to have my bags packed for the airport to return to Roanoke, Virginia. They, personally picked me up and drove me. A heavy oppression was brooding in the air. It was a long 17 mile trip as they said, "Larry, you were so good. We're going to miss you tremendously. We'll miss your talents." As they were trying to get me to talk, I didn't hear words, but blah blah blah sounds. I didn't say a damned thing for the entire 17 mile trip, all I could think of was—I just wanted to kill Johnny Johnson. It was a helpless anger that was simmering inside of me.

I was cut, in large part so that the Yankees could avoid paying a roster bonus. They had handed me a dark and relentless fate. The Yankees didn't want to pay the second half of the $2,500.00 they owed the Monarchs for buying out my contract. My shot at the big leagues was over. There I was leading the team, with one of the best arms in baseball and I got released. I just couldn't believe it when I got cut; neither did my teammates. I had finished my career barnstorming with Satchel Paige in 1964.

What was happening in the majors at the New York Yankees 1959 turf? Mickey Mantle and Bob Turley were exhibiting sub-par performance. Yogi Berra and Hank Bauer had one foot in the retirement seat. The American League champs would start slow and bounce only to the .500 mark. The year before? The National League imploded when two of New York's best teams, Brooklyn Dodgers and the Giants left the Big Apple for greener pastures and onto California. This left fans of the America's Pastime in a New York baseball deficit.

The St. Petersburg Times wrote, "The Front Office: It is with some embarrassment that the Saints obeyed the Yankees order to release LeGrande. The youngster had Negro league experience, arm, speed and power. Fans found the transaction hard to understand. LaGrande had been purchased from the Kansas City Monarchs on a conditional basis and a payment of $5,000.00 was due if he was retained beyond the 30 days. You could understand why the Yanks might not wish to pay it if they decided he wasn't a prospect. The Saints, however, may keep LaGrande anyhow. He has been released from the Yankee contract but he could be signed to a Saint pact. Problem: This might look like collusion to the Monarchs. At present, LaGrande is asking for permission to sign the Saint contract. If it's granted, the Saint outfield will be set."[41]

Four other teams were interested in signing me, just after I was cut by the Yankees, but it also planted the seeds of doubt in their minds. I believe they were afraid to sign me. They asked me questions such as: "Why did you get released? Did you get hurt? Did you do something wrong?"They eventually all shied away from me at that point—the Yankees had really messed up my career going forward and any chances thereafter to play in the major leagues. A dark time of disillusion followed and my ambition shivered into fragments.

Stan really felt horrible about the whole debacle and tried to get me a job to play in Canada. In retrospect, I'm glad it didn't pan out, because I wouldn't have been able to play with the Satchel Paige All Stars.

Stan Charnofsky sent me a letter dated June 11, 1960. The excerpt from the letter read:

> "Dear Larry, I have a recommendation for you, and that is that you try to write or contact someone in that new rookie league in Carolina. It belongs to the Continental League, and they are now looking for ballplayers to fill up their rosters. In fact, Paul Amann was just signed by one of the clubs up there. You are still considered a rookie, so if you could hook up with one of those teams, I feel you would have a good chance to show what you can do. Our club here has been in a bad slump, mostly because our hitting has been poor. Believe me, we could use a Larry LeGrande in our outfield right now.
>
> By the way, we had a little birthday party in your honor a couple of weeks ago, with a beautiful cake with your name written on it. All the guys were wishing you could have been here to share it with us.
>
> Hope all is well with you, and I, personally, want to wish you great success in baseball. I feel you are sincere about wanting to make it, and I think you have ability.
>
> Best of luck and personal regards,
> Stan Charnofsky"

But there was another angle to my being cut by the New York Yankees. Stan was fired on July 17, 1960, they claimed he had lost control of the team because the Saints had ended their season in last place. In an interview with the *St. Petersburg Times* Stan said, "I'm surprised, I feel the organization (New York Yankees) was satisfied: I am sure the pressure which brought this about, came from 'within'." The paper described Stan as having failed, through no fault of his own due to politics and side-swiping him with undermining tactics. The paper went on to say, "Stan Charnofsky began losing his job with the St. Petersburg Saints way back before he entered organized baseball. His fate was sealed the day the first major league mogul handed an untried high school boy a bundle of cash for signing a baseball contract." The newspaper described some of the newer Saints as nouveau rich kids that wanted everything handed to them on a silver platter and were very spoiled at best, not to mention extremely lazy on the field. They went on to say, "The stories about them are appalling enough without identities attached." They mentioned that they had broken all standards of training, and overall respect for the coaches and managers. "Meanwhile they have 'yessed' Charnofsky with a chilling condescension that was worse than rebellion and ignored much of what he tried to teach them." The paper went on to discuss my being cut for no reason at all other than I was part of the disrespectable bunch who weren't interested in playing baseball as I was. "Circle of Guilt: It is regrettable that the entire ballclub must be tarred with this brush when really, the majority of the players have been as shocked as you and I. Still, this majority did nothing to stop it. Individually they gawped in astonishment at the things they saw and waited for the hot dogs to meet their comeuppance. This never happened.

Instead, big bonus players continued to pose and frolic while players who were helping the club got the ax. For instance, Larry LeGrande, leading the team in average, total bases and runs-batted-in, and Dave Tucker, leading it in hustle, hit the road, told they were not major league prospects. When you fault Charnofsky, you must conclude he did not make this situation clear in the reports he sent streaming to the parent New York Yankees. Certainly a theory entertained here–that the Yanks would be content with any finish this year after the magnificent pennant teams of 1958 and 1959—proved to be wrong."[37]

I was sad, disappointed, disillusioned, confused and deceived. I had worked my baseball career and life since boyhood for over two decades with one goal: To play for the New York Yankees, even though other teams had wanted me to play for them—the Yankees had been number ONE in my sights. Now, in just moments, all of my dreams, goals and aspirations were ripped away. I was dumbfounded and really didn't know what to do next—I was shattered.

Soon after I received the letter from the NY Yankees, I was whisked away to the examination rooms to enter the military. I was in Fort Jackson, North Carolina and transferred to Fort Gordon, Georgia. It was there I started having back problems. I thought of my baseball career, but the back issues started to progress. I was then discharged from the service. In retrospect, to this day, I thank God I didn't go to Walter Reed Hospital. My friends weren't so lucky after their surgeries and ended up in wheelchairs. I would not have the mobility that I do today to attend tournaments and charity functions, and would have never barnstormed around the countryside with great players. The Vietnam War was raging from 1954 to 1975 as this country was in turmoil not only politically and socially, but had become a manifestation of the cold war between our country and the Soviet Union along with their allies. Although the United States got involved in 1964, this had been the longest and most controversial war. Many people were at odds with each other and families were separated. Some never returned from war. Marches and protests not only at our nation's capital, but on college campuses and public areas where demonstrators would risk their lives to put forth their opinions about stopping this terrible war.

Still, this was the Yankees with one of baseball's worst integration records. It didn't bring a black player up to its big-league club until Elston Howard elevated in 1955. Casey Stengel, the team's manager into the 1960's routinely referred to blacks as "niggers" and "jungle bunnies". Soon after Howard came up, Stengel announced, "When I finally get a nigger, I get the only one that can't run".

The Roanoke Times, former sports writer, Bill Brill had written an article entitled, "Baseball Deals Some Cruel Blows". He goes on to say, "Some things happen in baseball that don't seem quite fair." He goes on to write, "LeGrande proved to be the best outfielder the Saints had. He was hitting .304, was leading the league in triples and was tops on his club in RBI. He had shown good speed and power."[9]

The prominent box score printed in the *St. Petersburg Times*, listed the players in the league with all team players. My average was over .300 and I was in the top 10 percent of the league. My weekly wages with the Saints consisted of $175.00, after deductions of $26.55, my net take home was $148.45. It wasn't about the money, it was about the game.

There wasn't a doubt that I had proven myself and made good on the team as well as the league—I had just arrived at my twentieth birthday. But it would seem that the orders were followed by the St. Pete officials because they were only a farm club of the NY Yankees. So as in businesses, so it is in sports, the rules are made to protect the company. When a cut is made, the knife cuts deep and sometimes it never heals.

I thought the greatest thing in the world was when I signed with the Yankees. Looking back, I should have signed with one of the others because it was the biggest mistake I ever made. I ask God, to forgive me for the grudge I hold against Johnny Johnson, the Yankees Minor League Director for releasing me.

I had sent all my newspaper clippings back home to my family to read to show them how well I was playing. They knew how well I doing, so their expectations were extremely high to make it to the Yankees major league team.

Just after I was released I called home and spoke to my mother. My mother was devastated and in complete shock. She couldn't understand what had just happened. Out of her frustration, and without hesitation, she picked up the phone and called Johnny Johnson looking for answers. Mom demanded to know what was going on. Johnny, surprised that she called him, nervously said, "Well he's a great ball player, but we don't think he can hit the ball out of Yankee Stadium." My mother shouted, "What! What are you talking about? Larry has homerun power! Josh Gibson is the only one I know that hit one out of that park!" This was followed by nothing more than a very long pause. She hung up, frustrated with the non-response. Mom called me later on and agreed with me that she felt it was a racial issue because there was no other possible reason that I would be cut from the team.

Johnny's befuddled response was simply the dumbest answer I'd ever heard. Stan had me batting clean-up *(number*

4 in the line-up); because I had consistently earned the coveted status of power hitter for the team at the time of my release!

So later on, Ted Raspberry said, "That's OK, send Larry back to me I'll take him right off". So I came back to Roanoke for a couple of weeks, and then I went back to play for the Monarchs. The Scouts would ask me, "What the heck happened to you?" I never received closure for this. If I had gotten hurt, or I was getting into fights, I could see it, but I was a perfect gentleman and never had a cross word with anyone. I never got an official "pink slip", which they gave out at the time, so there was no documentation of my final release.

The year 1959 brought tragedy to the music industry where a chartered plane transporting our famous musicians Buddy Holly, Richie Valens, and our Big Bopper went down in an Iowa snowstorm killing all four. In the movies, *Ben-Hur* came on the scene in New York City and was the one of the most expensive films ever made aside from *Gone With the Wind* back in this timeframe.

In the majors, The Fall Classic saw the Los Angeles Dodgers defeat the Chicago White Sox, taking the series 4 games to 2 to become World Series Champs.

As for the country, John F. Kennedy defeated Nixon in 1960 and won the closest presidential election of the century. John F. Kennedy would go on to be one of the most recognized and beloved presidents of our time. In entertainment, our own Chubby Checker introduced the "Twist" at the famous Peppermint Lounge in New York City and Elvis Presley is discharged from the Army, returns home and immediately scores a series of hit singles and albums. In the majors, we saw the Pittsburgh Pirates defeat the Yankees 4 games to 3 to win the 1960 World Series with Bill Mazeroski's seventh game dramatic home run.

In other news, the Major League for 1960, the aging 70 year old Casey Stengel who was cracking under pressure with chest pains took a rest period for a few weeks, Mickey Mantle failed on a double-play and Roger Maris was hurt, but as season ended they did end up grabbing the American League pennant. Soon after Stengel got back on his feet his services were no longer required by the Yankees. Although, there were mixed opinions and reports of whether Stengel was deeply prejudicial, he had Elston Howard, and that was a beginning.

Barnstorming with
my Best Friend, Satch

The booking agents were the worst of all in terms of corruption. Satchel had found a map that Dempsey, one of our booking agents had. Satchel noticed the trips were all criss-crossed and very disorganized. It was no wonder we were exhausted the trips were not planned according to dates and locations to making it feasible in terms of logistics, and most importantly, rest. Dempsey was a white man and of course, he did not care, as he was getting a huge cut on all of the games we played. This is why we were traveling 300 and 400 miles in one trip. When Satch understood what was happening he said, "I'm going to talk to Ted Raspberry about this!" Things turned around very quickly. Thereafter, we were doing 75 to 100 miles after that; it was still a long day, but we loved our game. We played on average 75–80 ball games over a four-month road trip.

As Ted Raspberry began to form the Satchel Paige All-Stars 1960, Ted had filled Satch's roster rather quickly. Satch soon became disturbed by Ted's choices. Satch told Ted, "You better get better players, or else I'm staying here in Kansas City! *They have to be damned good!*"

I believe Satch chose me because I was one of those **damned good** players. *If you were better than me, you'd have to play like Willie Mays.*

One type of income was barnstorming tours, which provided the main source of livelihood. The tours pitted teams of Negro players against the best local talent during tours along the American countryside. The second venue, league play, offered structure, stability and a sense of belonging that barnstorming could not yield.

In 1958, we played in Saxton, Missouri. The Chamber of Commerce booked us and we played a local team. They rolled out the red carpet, and we beat them 14–0. When we first got there, we were at a restaurant, signed autographs and everything was great. We were meeting all kinds of local people and some had come from out of town to see us. After the game, we came back into the city, and found that all the restaurants were closed; we had no place to eat. So we went without dinner. MacAllister Keene, from Memphis, Tennessee was our driver. The loyalty and dedication of this man was second to none. When the team played, he slept so he could drive during the night to move our team to and from the baseball fields, or wherever our manager instructed the team to go to next. Sometimes, we would drive 400–500 miles from place to place almost every day or every couple of days. "Mac" had a saying on the bus, referring to the Bible, "live together and love one another," because this was racist times, and very difficult for black people. After the games, we still had to travel with our uniforms on. Whenever we spotted a small eatery near the railroad tracks, or off the beaten path, we would stop to eat. However, these places were almost as bad as the racist city restaurants. The hamburgers were 35 cents with 5 cents extra for a tomato. When our team would walk in and sit down at the tables, they said, "Don't pay any attention to those prices, they've changed". This was just another type of experience we would always encounter in our travels. We were given $2.00 a day for meal money. Typically, the hotdogs went from 0.15 to 0.30 cents after we piled out of the bus. When the owners in the diners would see us in uniform, the perception was—we had a lot of money.

The next day we were still in Missouri, played another local team, and beat them as well. We then went to Kansas City where Satchel and his wife, Lahoma (Lahoma Jean Brown) lived, and we checked into the hotel.

The hotel manager put us on the top floor, so the white staff could "keep an eye on us". There was a community bathroom at the end of the hall. Of course, by the time half the team got through their showers the bathtub was stopped up, but we just kept our showering, without complaining with water up to our knees. We didn't want to cause any trouble because they would have kicked us out of the hotel without a second thought.

The following day, Satchel came by the hotel and said that Lahoma was fixing a big dinner for the team. When we arrived at Satch's, we saw the dining room table with all the food. I said, "It was the first time I had seen a meatloaf that was two feet long and five inches wide and it looks like a huge cake with icing, but it was gravy." The team went nuts although they thought it was cake too, they dug into the meatloaf and raved about it for years. That day did turn out to be gravy; Satch and Lahoma were very gracious and big-hearted to open their home up to the entire team for the whole day.

I really loved Lahoma—she was such a nice lady and you could always talk to her about anything. She would sit, listen and understand, but most of all, she'd give you sound advice. She would talk to us about how to budget: How much money to take on the road and how much to send home. She also had a great sense of humor. I was young, and she was always there to talk to because I was away from home so much and so often. Her cheering smile and laughter would always pick me up.

They were on East 28th Street with a huge living room-dining room area. The dining room chairs had huge backs on them, the likes we had never seen before and people just went there to kick their shoes off, relax and have a good time talking about good times, baseball and especially family. They had beautiful furniture that many people had given Satchel over the years. There was a baby Grand Piano in the living room and this was where the dining room was and where the team ate together. The team was finally off for three days, so it was much like a mini vacation at Satchel's house. Satchel's drink of choice was Old Charter whiskey, and sometimes he would drink it with beer. In another corner was a huge picture of famous people, and Satchel's picture was in the center along with his wife, Lahoma. There were large photos of movie stars, famous people and celebrities that Satchel had met and worked with. Among some of the people were Gregory Peck, Roosevelt, as well as Robert Mitchum—alongside where Satchel was a co-star in a movie. After the 1957 season, Satch went to Durango, Mexico to appear in a movie called *"The Wonderful Country"*, by United Artists, the stars were Robert

Mitchum and Julie London. Satch had played Sergeant Tobe Sutton, a hard-bitten Union army cavalry sergeant of a segregated black unit. He was paid $10,000.00 and the movie became the one of the great prides of his life.

Satchel said, "Hey Larry! Come on downstairs!" As I made my way to the very large finished room downstairs he started to show me his carbine rifle. One part of his basement downstairs was finished and the other part was not, it was slate rock. He had hung a large shooting target in the basement approximately twenty feet away. He proceeded to pick up the rifle and *BANG!* Next thing we heard was Lahoma yelling downstairs, "*Satchel!*" Satchel retorted with a resounding, "You take care of that, and I'll take care of this". He then turned to me and said, "All right Larry, it's your turn". The chips and slate were flying everywhere. Satchel and I laughed to our hearts content. There was a house full of people and we continued with our target practice. The team remained upstairs with no comment or shouting down the stairs. The team said nothing about the two shooters in the basement target practicing with a high-powered rifle. I felt the recoil up against my shoulder, but we just kept on. We decided to return to the gathering upstairs. We passed by Lahoma and she gave Satchel a dirty look and rolled her eyes without further words. All the teammates were stuck together as one. They were telling jokes, stories and laughing. We all got along famously, and none of them were upset or put out over Satch and I target-practicing in the basement or any other events that we had together—they understood our friendship was based on sportsmanship and hunting.

Satch's children were always well-behaved and proper. I remember Satch who loved fishing and hunting so much, that he had the kids pick one of these activities—so most of them chose fishing. They went fishing and fishing and fishing! The kids enjoyed their time with their father catching fish and his love.

The team got back on their bus from out of Kansas City the next day from Satchel's house, and I remained behind with George Chin Davis (who played on the Kansas City Monarchs from 1960–1961). Satchel came over to the hotel and picked George and I up for the trip. We proceeded to Nebraska and the red carpet rolled out for us. We were playing a local team at the time. The local team showed up and began taking the field. The pitcher and catcher came to the plate, but their face and arms were jet black—they had painted their faces and arms with black pitch, this being 1958. Satchel said to me, "I've never seen anything like this in my entire baseball career." Satchel then said to the umpire, "If they don't take that stuff off, we're going to leave immediately!" The tar-skinned figures left the field and returned to play the game. We finished the game and hit the road once again. So we're going down the highway and returned to Kansas. The windows were rolled down and it was 95 degrees, Satchel was in the back seat with his pants rolled up drinking his bottle of Old Charter, happy as a lark. Nevertheless, we were ready for yet another game when we returned a couple of days later.

I recall one of the most interesting stories that Satch told me. Satch pitched in the 1930's for a businessman in South Dakota who owned a Cadillac dealership. Satch was living in a boxcar at the time in Bismark. In our barnstorming days, thirty years later, his friend had us come back up to Bismark to play a local team. His friend gave Satch a .22 rifle while we were visiting and the next day I went to the hardware store and bought a box of .22 shells for the gun. Because South Dakota was known as the "pheasant state," There were pheasants and jackrabbits every where. On our way out of Bismark, we saw a drove of jackrabbits. I said, "Let's pull over and get some food!" So we pulled over and I knocked off one of the jackrabbits. We continued on down the road, we saw some pheasants. I said, "Satch, pull over again!" The pheasants started to scramble and elude us in the tall grassy field. I had my eye on one, pulled the trigger and supper was complete.

We stopped at the edge of town, to fix our dinner. As I pulled out our Coleman stove and the catch, Satch says to me, "Do you know what to do?" I said, "Ya, 'cus you don't!" But we both knew and just laughed it off.

Just as dinner was ready to eat, a little white kid comes up on his bicycle. Satch looked at me and said, "Here comes trouble!" The little boy said, "Where are you guys from?" Satch answered, "Lots of places!" The little boy got on his bicycle and left. Satch then said, "The police will be showing up pretty soon." Not 15 minutes later, sure enough, there they were. The police came over to us and said, "What are you doing man!?" Satch said, "Travelin'! 175 miles out to play baseball." The police then said, "Where are you headed?" Satch rarely looked people in the eye when they spoke to him. As the police would continue to talk Satch would look at the trees and the sky. Then the police turned to me and asked, "What's your name son?" I replied, "Larry LeGrande, sir." He turned to Satch and asked, "What's your name?" Satch simply replied, "Paige." At that moment, the officer walked back to his car and when he returned with a pen and paper he then asked Satchel to sign it!" Next thing we knew 30 more people came out to see us to get autographs. Somehow word got around fast. But all these people made us late getting to the ballgame.

My expedition with Satchel proved that Satchel could pitch better and better with each game that passed. Before the game Satchel would take a bat, draw a line and simply paint the corners. Satchel stayed on the corners every single time he played. His most important pitch was the fastball, but he was also known for inventing the ingenious hesitation pitch in 1943. By the 1950's he was throwing every fast ball you could imagine, along with the screwball, knuckleball and the eephus pitch (a low velocity pitch that catches the hitter off guard most of the time). Sometimes called the nothing pitch, its origins come from Hebrew meaning "nothing". This particular pitch is thrown overhand with an arc of about 25 feet high. This usually appears to move in slow motion in the area of 40–50 mph versus the typical fast pitch of 80–100 mph. Today, we sometimes call this special pitch the balloon ball, blooper ball, gondola, parachute or the rainbow pitch. Most of all, what set him apart from other pitchers was his mastery of control. My friend was known to pitch over a gum wrapper.

These days as I fondly review photos of my dear departed friend, I can see the intensity in his face. I said to myself, I know what he's thinking...*this is a strikeout.*

I was chatting with Tom LaSorda at one point, during a charity event, that he should get a video of Greg Maddox to see how he pitches because he never threw the ball much over 90 mph, but he threw bullets with pinpoint accuracy. Greg Maddox does remind me of how Satchel played the game because Greg would throw the ball down the plate or paint the corners at will. If Greg wanted a pitch one inch off the outside corner of the plate at the knees—he could do it. Although he didn't throw as hard as Satch, he had great control. This is why Satchel was so great—control, control,

control. Today, I believe the coaches are instructing the players to throw in the 90's and its all show, with all speed. Sometimes, I watch the game these days and I hate the way they play ball today. All they try to do is find a player that can throw over 90 mph, instead of finding someone with a good change up, good accuracy and control. With these three things, you could easily win many more ball games.

In 1960, when I finally got back to the family farm, there was a letter, sitting on the table addressed to my parents. To my surprise, and my parents' astonishment, Topps Chewing Gum had sent a letter to my parents for a baseball agreement to add my picture in the "Annual Topps Baseball" picture card series just after I completed my season with the Monarchs. They needed parental permission, of course because I was under twenty-one at the time.

*This...*I thought to myself. ***This, is absolute fame AND they're advertising me—everyone would know who Larry LeGrande is.*** My parents approved and I jumped for the chance.

Courtesy of Larry LeGrande. Topps letter requesting Larry LeGrande's photo in the annual Topps Baseball Picture Card Series

The letter was requesting consent from parents to use my photo in the annual Topps Baseball Picture Card Series. My mother had showed that letter to every one I our church, friends and grocery stores. She was so proud to receive the letter.

To this day, I'm so proud of that letter as well as what my mother had done and said about me in the community. *I felt, important AND famous!*

The greatest satisfaction I got from playing with Satchel, was the first day that I called him and listened to him tell me about all the things he did in the game of baseball and not by reading in the newspapers. Also, it was great to be around him and to learn about his every day life and how he viewed it. Satchel was a self-made ballplayer. I would not have done anything different playing with Satch. I think everything was perfect when we were on and off the field and I have no regrets. Satch was all business when he put his uniform on. But enjoyed sharing stories about the games, travels from state to state and of course, women. The women swooned over the ballplayers where ever he was and where ever the teams played, whether it be on the field or off. The only thing I miss to this day, is that we didn't have cameras or video cameras like they do today. I can only hold my memories of him and share them here in this writing.

Satch truly had the greatest eye-hand control of anyone I've ever seen. When he arrived at the plate, he drew a line with his bat. His focus was second-to-none.

Satchel always could "thread the needle" in his pitch. I recall the game where Jimmy Piersall called Satch the "N-word". Satch never said a word, but pitched the ball right under Jimmy's armpit just as he lifted his bat. *Swish!* The ball went right past Piersall, before he could get his bat down. Satch later said to me, "I felt like I wanted to kill him with the ball," because Satch later told the team that, "Piersall had been calling me the N-word for quite some time.". Satch said, "That was the only person I wanted to kill in my life". We've all had that feeling at one time or another, that fleeting moment of hatred and anger that takes over, then the human control and common sense takes over.

Today, they want you to throw with extreme speed. For example, in 2002, Don Baylor was managing the Chicago Cubs and Mark Prior had the St. Louis Cardinals three to nothing in the seventh inning. The pitch count reached, which is the stupidest thing, in my opinion, because I feel it is the fans that are being cheated. Don Baylor pulled him out and put in Jeff Fessaro and the first pitch he sent Mark McGuire through it out of the ballpark. He pulled Fessaro out and the short stop for the Cardinals hit the home run and the Cubs lost the ballgame. In my time, we went as 'hard as you can, and as long as you can' that is the way you play baseball—it was all about stamina. I know that the pitch count is all about saving arms today, but they have their gymnasiums, good foods, vitamin supplements and the best sports doctors and we were very lucky to get a bologna sandwich and a couple of fried eggs.

Courtesy of Larry LeGrande. Copy of original letter
from Satchel Paige to Larry LeGrande.

Satchel wrote me a letter *requesting ME* to join and play for the Satchel Paige All-Stars. I thought to myself, *there couldn't be much better other than making it to the majors than to make it on the Satchel Paige All-Star team.*

As the 1960's came around, I decided to barnstorm the countryside with my good friend, Satch and his Satchel Paige All-Stars. The hunting and fishing was an extravaganza type of trip before, during and after our barnstorming era. I played in Canada with the Satchel Paige All-Stars. We really, thoroughly, enjoyed playing with and against the Canadians. There was no discrimination, racial segregation or tension.

I received a hand-written letter from my friend and I read it a hundred times, Satch was requesting I join the Satchel Paige All-Stars. Something noteworthy, however, in all the news clippings, announcements and letters from my friend Satch, they had always spelled his name with one *L* (Satchel), in his hand-written letters to me he'd always sign his name with two *l*s (Satchell). Funny thing is, although everyone spelled his name with one *L*, Satchel, signed it with two *LL's*, *Satchell.*

Satch said, "Bring a uniform and a glove if you have one." He could only pay $150.00 a week. But I would have taken anything from him just to play with him. I learned a lot about the baseball business on and off the field.

We played together here and there in 1958 to 1959—it was one of the best times of my life and was certainly an honor. Then starting barnstorming with him until 1964. I was overjoyed and thrilled to get the letter to play on the All-Star team. It was the most fun I ever had playing baseball and that includes the Yankees' Winter League. Nevertheless, I wanted to go where Elston Howard was. Elston Howard played with the Kansas City Monarchs but did not come to the Yankees through their minor league system; he went through the Kansas City Athletics. When he came, it was in a trade with Roger Maris. I always said that Yogi Berra was a good catcher too and I just wanted to go back because he used to kick the Dodgers' butts and besides, he was a great man.

The toughest group I ever had to get cooperation from was in the Satchel Paige All-Stars within the Negro Leagues. Some had ability and talent and some did not. We were in spring training, with the world's greatest pitcher. The meeting came together at the hotel room, and we felt we had a sense of urgency to be top performers on the spot. Satchel did send some folks home because they just were not ready, or they did not have the ability.

The Satchel Paige All-Star team always got along famously together and never had any incidents. However, one day we did experience a fight that broke out in Pennsylvania with a truckload of white men calling the team names and screaming obscenities at us. They were being extremely aggressive and loathsome and of course using the "nigger" word. Until one of the players yelled out, *"Stop!"* The white men got out of vehicle after circling the hotel several times, looking for a fight. One of the players knocked out two of the white perpetrators, and our pitcher knocked out another white man, then I proceeded to slam the door on them. The police showed up shouting, "Leave the team alone!" They commanded the white folks to leave the area immediately. Witnesses informed the police, so that our exploits were not misinterpreted. I always felt the team bonded together because there was such a genuine respect for one another personally and professionally.

I also knew that the respect the players gleaned from each other was from standing together against racism and forging a strong bond, friendship and camaraderie amongst ourselves.

By November of 1963, America experienced a blow they would never forget—the assassination of President Kennedy. JFK was not only a Democratic President and Roman Catholic, but was a strong supporter of the civil rights movement at the time when the country needed him the most. His speeches typically consisted of peace and the man is the beginning and the end of mutual tolerance, that any problems man has created can be solved by man. He also believed in eliminating racial segregation because "it disturbs the national conscience". It devastated the fabric of this country where we would all be at a great loss from a great leader. It was very difficult to understand for blacks and whites alike, but Satch kept his eye on the ball and kept his All-Stars focused and motivated for the next game.

The Satchel Paige All-Stars played in the Menasha Ballpark one Saturday in June of 1963. The *Osh Kosh Daily Northwestern* announced our Satch as "immortal" in the upcoming game against the Macs. They went on to say, "Leroy 'Satchel' Paige now in his 38th season of ball playing, has assembled his own club for the first time and it taking them on a coast to coast barnstorming tour. The club's line-up comprised of major league hopefuls will include Satchel Paige or one of his younger counterparts on the mound with Isaac Walker behind the plate. At first base will be Henry Meyers while Oscar Walker holds down second Manning the shortstop position will be Billy Moore, with Willie Washington on third base. In the outfield will be Larry LeGrande at left field, Jason Stallings at center and Fred Greens at right field."[19]

We were having a good day in the great state of Wisconsin against the Menasha Macs. The *Osh Kosh Daily Northwestern* stated, "Larry LeGrande started off the scoring battle in the first inning when he came in on Fred Green's double to put the tally at 1–0 for the Stars." The Macs were 2–1 in the second, we pulled in two runs in the third. The Macs had piled up four runs in the fifth and the tally was at 6–3. The sixth and seven innings were a bust for us with no runs. By the eight inning, Satch took over the mound and fanned Mac's Keller for third out. The ninth inning found us neck in neck 7–7 typing up the scoring with my buddies Greene and Washington. The paper went on to say that Satch, "then retired the Macs in four batters, giving up no hits. The Mac lineup was changed in the tenth inning with Clem Massey hurling and Phil Keller behind the plate. The Star's Anderson had made his way to third base when catcher Keller missed the pitch allowing Anderson to put the score at 8–7 for the Stars."[20]

Barnstorming with Satchel and the rest of the players was not only fun being together and enjoying each other company while touring the states and the provinces, but it was also incredibly stressful mentally and physically. They were forced to go barnstorming for financial reasons. They did not make a lot of money to sustain themselves and their families so they had to take their expertise on the road. At least with the barnstorming tours, we were paid every day with Satch. I averaged $30.00 to $40.00 a day.

I recall a conversation with Lahoma, Satchel's wife on their financial woes, and she told me that she had "Never seen anyone get cheated out of their money as Satchel did." The only time he made decent money was back in 1946 in the Negro Leagues and in the AAA divisions. There were no retirement programs back then, so when a player retired or stopped playing—that was it, they were on their own for any future income. An event to note in 1946, the Negro Leagues began integration of their own accepting Eddie Klep as the first white player to play for the Cleveland Buckeyes during their season.

Satch still pitched three innings a night—every night.

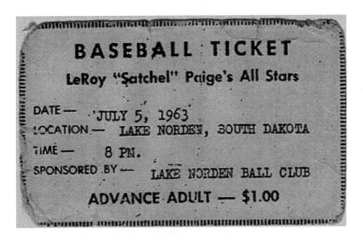

Courtesy of Larry LeGrande. Copy of original
game ticket for the Satchel Paige All-Stars.

I recalled a story of Satchel talking to his teammates. He was kidding and joking with us and always said that he, "Wanted us to do the right thing". He told his teammates and some sport writers about visiting my family's farm. He said, "Larry's cattle is so poor, you could hang your hat on them for a damned hat rack". The sports writers were there, talking to Satch saying, "Where's Larry!?" They pointed to my head and everyone laughed. He was a great joke teller and a good storyteller. He had time for everybody: Sports writers, fans, and VIPs. He often said, "I could work for anyone in baseball, but I just don't have the education." He always spoke about not being in the Baseball Hall of Fame, but I always told him that they would find a place for him.

Satch and I would be in a nightclub somewhere and after talking to a would-be player he would say, "See him? I'll pick him to play. He better be good to play with 'ole Satch, 'cus he won't play on my team!" He certainly knew how to pick 'em.

One night as we were coming out of a night club, I saw Satch's wallet laying on the seat in the automobile, so I looked in the wallet, I had found several birth cards with different dates on them, which I thought amusing and so did Satchel. When Satch got in the car, I asked him if I could borrow the $20.00 bill that was in his wallet. Satch reached for his wallet, he said, "How did you know I had $20.00?" I said, "I found all these birth cards with different dates on them." Satch said, "No one knows exactly when I was born!" We had a good laugh about it.

Not having his wallet in the bar, was never a problem. One thing I can say about those white people in the bar, we never had to pick up a tab—the drinks were always on the house. As the bar would close, Satch would ask for a bottle of Old Charter, his drink of choice as well as the team's. The bartender would wrap the bottle so we could take it back to the hotel and continue drinking because we would have the following day off as there were no games to play. Even though the alcohol laws were stretched, the bartenders were more than happy to oblige Satch as we socialized in the bars.

During my barnstorming days with Satch, there was one hot afternoon as we were warming up and Satch noticed that the plate was "too big", so I placed a hot dog wrapper down on the ground as home plate. Satch then shouted, "Hey, that's too big too, so we used a gum wrapper." You can bet, and as I witnessed my friend Satch, he fired it in right over the gum wrapper as it lay. All you had to do was set a target and he would find it. He was that good. I cherished the chance to play with Paige.

The Negro leagues were dead. The black teams that survived for a while were the barnstormers—taking on all the comers. Satch could really pack the fans in. In a town of 10,000 people there would be 20,000 in attendance.

Satchel Paige, was a great American baseball player known for his wit, extremely good sense of humor and extraordinary pitching ability. He became legendary while barnstorming in the Negro baseball leagues prior to the integration (1947) of the major leagues. Satchel was born in Mobile Alabama, but no one knows for sure when he was born, exactly, some guess 1906. They didn't keep many records on negro individuals in the early 1900's. He played in approximately 2,500 games, won approximately 2,000 and credited with more than 300 shut-outs and 55 no-hitters. In 1948, we are guessing, around the age of forty-two, he joined the Cleveland Indians of the American League. He pitched for six seasons in the majors and was the first star pitcher of the Negro leagues to be inducted (1971) into the Baseball Hall of Fame. Satch could strike out fifteen to eighteen batters per game. In his thirty-year career he had played for the Birmingham Black Barons, Pittsburgh Crawfords, the Kansas City Monarchs, New York Black Yankees and others. He played in the Caribbean during the off season. Not surprisingly, one of his fast-balls was clocked at 103 mph. Satch was right-handed, tall and lanky about 6-foot 4-inches and would always say, "Don't look back, something might be gaining on you." Most people got a kick out of his sayings.

In a book entitled *Satchel Paige and Company*, they wrote, "Former teammate and catcher Larry LeGrande, has said that Satchel would field ground balls at third base and look into the opposite team's third-base dugout. He would throw perfectly to first base, on the money, while still looking into the dugout and never looking at first base."[11]

As a boy, Satch, went to work at the Mobile, Alabama train station. Mobile being his place of birth he became an enterprising sort. He was born Leroy Robert Paige on July 7, 1906. He hustled the train traveler's luggage for tips. He soon learned that if he fixed up a rig to carry more luggage he'd get more tips. He earned the name "Satchel Tree" since shortened to Satchel.

I was nearing the end of the season and my last stretch with the Kansas City Monarchs and Satch in August of 1964. We were playing the Twins City Twins in Benton Harbor, Michigan. *The News Palladium* went on to write, "Fans arrived promptly at the Riverfront Park Thursday waited for four hours to see Satchel take the mound, but the aging wonder needed only seven pitches to preserve a 4–2 victory." We had mechanical problems with the bus and had to make stop, but finally made it to the game almost two hours late. The Twins' pitcher, "Price gave up five hits and two walks in the first three innings, but was bailed out twice by sharp fielding plays." The Twins' Stouffer, center, "threw a bull's-eye to second base to kill an attempted double steal in the first, and Daniels was nailed in a run down in the second when the Monarchs got their lone earned run on Larry Doster's double and Jone's single. Price would up with 10 strikeouts and six-hitter allowing only one single in the final six innings…but the damage had been done."[22]

In this incredible game against the Twins, I had 4 at bats, 2 hits, 1 run batted in and 1 triple with no runs. Satch was still a sight to see in this game. He enjoyed amusing fans not only on the mound, but also behind the Monarch's dugout.

The year 1964 was interesting in politics, sports and entertainment. In the majors, The St. Louis Cardinals edge the New York Yankees in the World Series 4 games to 3. The Beatles came to U. S. soil to entertain us on the Ed Sullivan show.

President Johnson signed the infamous medicare bill and last but not least, our beloved Dr. Martin Luther King won the Nobel Peace Prize.

The Nobel Peace Prize awarded to the young, Dr. King was a game changer for society. His faith-based speech hinged on the powerful, biblical core of turning the other cheek and his undying life's devotion to the struggle for Negro rights in this country.

Barnstorming with the Canadians

In 1960, we began playing in Canada. The Canadians welcomed the Negro teams warmly, there was no racism there, and they loved American baseball as well as all the players no matter what race they were. The *Winston-Salem Journal* spoke to me in 2003 where I stated, "The best places to play were in the north—the Dakotas and the five provinces of Canada. We were treated like kings." I shared the racism challenges that we faced with the Journal. "The thrill of victory was sometimes overshadowed by the agony of racism. Defeat didn't sit well in some towns. After losses, the local inns would sometimes run out of rooms. Or there might be a 'hint' that the winning team should hit the road. Immediately."[5]

During a ride to British Columbia, Canada, Satch was commenting, "What a great pitch a knuckleball is!" I was looking out the window, not paying attention to Satch. He said, "Larry! I'm talkin' to you!" I said, "I'm looking at this huge grizzly bear and her two cubs!" I had never seen a bear before and they were something to see. Then Satch insisted I listen to him, he said, "I want to talk to you about the knuckleball!" He claimed he didn't need it because he was striking out 14-15 hitters a game, but he did admit that "it's a mean pitch!" He said "You know, the umpire can't call it, the catcher can't catch it, the batter can't hit it, the pitcher can't throw it—so, you see? I tell you it's a bitch!"

Satch was always as comical as Redd Foxx, the comedian. Many times when we'd pass places with 200–500 miles to travel; I would be driving and Satchel would say, "Slow down there's a bar, let's go check out what's going on in there!" We would go in, and joke with people jump back in the car and continue on our many journeys.

In our barnstorming tours across Canada, we never lost to them. We couldn't lose to them, because the news would travel fast that we lost. Otherwise, nobody would come to the games. So we had to be the best in our game, so they'd want to play us. If you were gonna play for Satch you had to be better than good. If you didn't play up to your expectations, then you were gone. Satch said, "I worked 42 years for my name and ain't nobody gonna tear it down—but me."

We barnstormed Canada for about three years, and the crowd was always large, they were wonderful and they were welcoming. We saw no racism. The money was good and we got paid every day. I love Canada!

Satchel could throw the ball wherever he wanted to. He surely painted the corners even as he got much older. Many pitchers nowadays, throw hard, but none of them can pitch as he did. He struck out more batters than anyone I ever knew. I was playing in the Satchel Paige All- Stars for four seasons. Most of the team owners owned sporting houses and the numbers racket. Ted Raspberry, with the exception of the Martin brothers started the second Satchel Paige All-Stars. Some of the sporting houses were much like brothels back in the day—originally. Satchel wanted to start the All-Stars to begin with.

We would sit and talk together with Satchel some days, and some of the other players visibly, did envy me. Satchel would sit there, point at me, and say, "I pick him to play with me on my team." He had better be good 'else he can't play on my team." To this day, I believe God gave me the ability, and my brother gave me the drive and motivation to start playing at fourteen years old.

I love to follow good baseball players and the Dodgers won in 1955 and the Braves in 1957, which is why I may have signed with them. I could have signed with them or the Milwaukee Braves, the Detroit Tigers, Washington Senators, the Cleveland Indians or the White Sox. But, I wanted to play for the Yankees. They had Elston Howard and Mickey Mantle and I just wanted to play there. If the Giants had wanted to sign me, I would have played with Willie Mays— who was my idol. I could have signed with the Braves or the Indians and I would have made a career out of it. But, I wanted to play with the best because I was a good ball player. I was so pissed off and mad at Johnny Johnson, I felt that I'd rather play with a local team than those sorry teams. I made a decision that forfeited my career in a sense. I tell my retired friends who did play with the Braves and the Indians that *"I wanted to play with the best"* and that I'd be retired from the team I signed with just out of loyalty. I was that cocky, but in retrospect, this was good back then. I ended up staying home for a couple of weeks then returned back to the Monarchs.

Once I returned, I was tearing up the league. The major league scouts were attending these games and they asked about me every night. The common comment was, "What in the world is he doing back here on this team?!" As I kept hearing this, it was a *ringing endorsement* of what I knew was true—I was good enough for the major leagues.

I recall a night, approaching dusk, when the bus driver was pulled over in Louisville, Kentucky because he didn't have the right state tag. The police made us follow him to an impoundment lot. The entire team was locked up along with the bus behind a six-foot tall chain link fence. They kept us until 7:30 p.m. The game was to start promptly at 7:00 p.m. There were 20,000 people waiting for us, and nobody knew where we were. We dressed inside the bus, got released and sped to the ballpark. Most times we had to change on the bus, because there was nowhere else to get changed or local establishments wouldn't allow us in the buildings.

Every day brought forth a highlight when I was asked, "What was the highlight in playing with Satchel Paige?" I remember a day like it was yesterday in Louisville, Kentucky, where we were having breakfast. He ordered ham and eggs. The waitress brought him the eggs but the eggs were too hard, and the ham was overcooked and hard. He sent the ham and eggs back five times. Then the manager came out and the coffee was too strong. Satch took a $100.00 bill out of his pants pocket and paid for it. You should have seen everyone's faces—some were shocked and some were grinning ear-to-ear.

We played a game in Kentucky in a cow pasture outside of Louisville. We had over 19,000 people watching the game on a Saturday. The following day, on that Sunday we played in Yankee Stadium. From a cow pasture in Kentucky one day to Yankee Stadium the next.

I remember playing a game in Kentucky where everything depended on me in the moment. The game was tied. Rain had just finished pouring down; some of the players were slipping and sliding in the mud. I started to field the ball and when I put my glove up, I lost my footing and suddenly, the ball hit me in the chest causing us to lose the game. The smack on my chest sounded like a bass drum and felt even worse. If you could have seen Satchel looking at me with that cold stare, it would have given you the shivers on a hot, steamy day. He shouted at me, "Why you didn't catch that damned ball!?" I said, "Satch, you saw me lose my footing". He said, "Lose! Hell! Ya shoulda caught that!" I was well aware that Satch had very high expectations of me. Lose? Me? ...Anybody but me! I did lose a few at bat, but I also won quite a few bat too—it's thrilling remembering those times at bat.

We would play rain or shine. Our livelihood depended on it. We never had rainouts—we had to play. As long as we got at least four innings in, we got paid. Many of us would get groin injuries from slipping in the mud. On occasion, they would pour gasoline on the field and burn it to dry out the land to avoid injuries. We went to any means to play ball even if it meant to prep the field. You had to love baseball—*and we needed to eat!*

Off the field, Satchel was a very sharp dresser. He wore double-breasted suits and wings tipped shoes. Although he never took the whole team out for dinner, we still enjoyed his company off the field. He loved to gamble now and then and sometimes we'd join him.

I noticed over the course of a half dozen times or so, that Satchel would make me turn around as we had started on one of our road trips out of town and we had to go back to the house or the hotel because Satchel had forgotten his 'tooth'. I got so used to him feverishly patting his suit coat pockets, I immediately recognized the situation. The breaks would go on whether I was driving the bus or in the car. I pulled over and headed back, many times, 30 miles or more to the place where he had left his partial. I remember one time, where I ran back into the hotel and the front desk manager had Satch's tooth wrapped up in a napkin waiting for its owner. So now we were 90 miles out of our way—it was just par for the course with Satch. We'd laugh it off and continued on down the road. These forgetful events would typically happen when we were off the next day with no ballgame scheduled. We would spend too much time in the nightclub. We couldn't put the blame on Satch because we had all painfully crawled out of the sack in the morning and no one thought to ask Satch if he had his tooth.

One day Satchel had broken his artificial tooth and got quite upset, although he carried an epoxy, because it had happened before. Satch said, "You're my fishing and hunting buddy! I know you can fix a rifle good, so you can fix teeth!"

He handed it to me to mend, as we finally made our way back to Kansas City. Satchel finally was able to get impressions made for a new set of teeth. Satch continued to eat whatever he pleased such as apples, peanuts…and he'd break the partial again and again. Satch had his children fix his teeth when he was at home. It was just a way of life for the kids.

Satchel and I would take turns driving the car on the road trips and take turns with some of the teammates on the bus. Whoever drove the car had the map and sometimes we would average 300 miles a day from baseball game to baseball game.

Satchel loved to play cards and one of his favorites was Hearts. He would play this with me for hours and some of the teammates until we fell asleep on the long road trips. He hated to lose at Hearts, he was so competitive and held himself in high standards when competing in anything. He would generally win most of the time.

Satchel and I continued our hunting excursions all over the country especially in the midwest and northwest areas as well as in some Canadian provinces. We went fishing in Canada together and found some excellent fishing spots with the help of the Cree Indians.

The Cree people inhabited the northwest regions of Canada. We enjoyed them because as Satch and I loved hunting they were also hunters and sometimes they acted as guides as we hunted through the areas. They were happy to show us baseball players where the good fishing was and it was helpful for both parties to explore each other's culture and what we had in common—eating from Mother Nature's table.

Satchel and I barnstormed in Canada often and enjoyed ourselves immensely as discrimination was almost non-existent there. We played against the Canadian ballplayers and were welcomed with open arms each time the American players went to the 'Great White North' to play baseball. I always said that the Canadians were the best people we had ever met in our entire life.

Back in the day, the Canadians had bars with escort services. If the players had an escort, they could get into the bars or bar restaurants. The bars looked just like apartment buildings with two front doors. "Men Only" on the left side and "Men and Women" on the right side. There were no singles to avoid confusion and fights over women. To get into the right door, you had to be with an female escort or as a couple. We would enter on the "Men Only" side, and we were always served two tall glasses each of beer with 14 percent alcohol at 0.25 cents a glass.

They were almost like our private clubs today; the only difference was the players could not experience their types of entertainment possibilities back in the United States.

The fans of baseball love to complain all the time that they don't play the game like they used to. I know this for a fact. I played the game and I was good at it. One of the things that I can't understand about today's players is that they have the ability, but not the initiative to learn fundamentals and they make too many mental mistakes. They're all strong, well-built young men, who lift weights to hit home runs. Yet they continue to hurt themselves in practice and playing the game. Pitchers make more errors and do more overthrowing because they are trying to throw the ball harder than what they need to and then they are missing the plate with a lack of accuracy. For instance, I was watching a game the other day on television and observed this: Freddy Garcia for the Mets, was pitching against the Cardinals. The catcher called for an outside pitch and Garcia threw the ball inside, the batter hit it out of sight.

The pitchers throw hard, but they can't throw to the target and if they throw it over the heart of the plate—it's why there's so many home runs. It's the old saying. "The harder you throw it, the harder I hit it."

Today's millionaire players occasionally will meet the old-time Negro Leaguers and shake our hands, hug us and tell us, "I appreciate you for opening the door." Then, they leave it at that. They have no idea how much we are suffering in our elderly retirement, in some cases dire poverty and failed health. I tell them the Negro leagues were the most famous leagues that God ever gave man. We played real baseball, and I'm proud to be a part its history.

Some companies today are exploiting some of the Negro League ball players for their own selfish benefits. In a one-way street attitude, many times they don't provide the families with royalties because they feel the players are gone, or not in good health or without their faculties. They have been exploiting my friend, Satch's pictures in different events, spectacles, and museums and public venues. Most of the time, venues do not think of inviting the negro baseball veterans to host or honor them. Some of the elderly veterans cannot afford healthcare, even less any trips across the country. For example, when the Obamas were in Kansas City at their typical photo op, none of my friends in the Negro leagues were invited to attend. I personally and a couple of my friends, did not hear of it until many weeks later.

America lost Satchel June 5, 1982 of emphysema and heart failure. Although we all smoked and drank in this era, many didn't live to a ripe old age. We were smoking Pall Mall cigarettes all the time and eventually this took Satchel away from us. He had passed away from—emphysema, and now I share Satchel's final years of suffering and pain—I own the disease as he did. Even though Satch frequently said, "You can't follow me, cus I don't know which way I'm going." It was truly a great loss to me as well as my family.

Proudly, Satch was voted into the Baseball Hall of Fame in 1971. This was a terrible loss for me personally, he was much like a brother to me. We shared a lot of secrets and many stories especially when we were hours and hours on the road together. This was some of the best quality time I had with Satch—we could laugh like crazy, but we had our serious talks about baseball, the management, the owners and our families.

Satch and I knocked down the miles and the teams we challenged along the way, from Nebraska through Wyoming, Canada and back to Kansas City—with all types of venues in which players displayed their talents.

The end of the barnstorming with Satchel and I came to a very sad close in 1964. The black players were getting scholarships in the white universities; this killed the playing talent, in a matter of speaking. They went to school, but they weren't playing at the same time and weren't practicing. This was a bittersweet end to the Negro Leagues.

I was thankful to God in my latter days that I ended up being Satchel's right-hand man—off the field as well as on. I don't need to brag about this, but he loved my abilities to play baseball, my physical power and agility. It was everything that Satchel admired. I could run fast and he was enamored with four teams wanting to sign me in 1959. I had to be good, if you think about it, I started at fourteen years old playing baseball with guys that were more than 12 years older than I was. I ended my baseball career with the Satchel Paige All-Stars!

Fans, Fans, Fans and Danger

Beneath the cold glare of the desolate night I've recalled women on our road trips. We were after all, sports figures and Satchel was famous in his travels and exploits. Women were everywhere when we played our games, they wanted to meet us and demanded to be taken out as they saw us as celebrities with money. There was a thing called "5 and 2" the women wanted $2.00 for sex and you had to pay $5.00 for the motel room. This happened with the Negro Leagues as well as Satch's teams. Some found time to be with the women at night if they had the energy and stamina especially after sleeping on the bus during the tours. We had to go to the bathroom in the woods, without the white folk seeing us because we'd get arrested if we were caught. Not one time did the police stop us in our tours. The women were not allowed on any of our bus trips. However, there was a time or two when we allowed a couple of them to get on the bus just for a short trip across the city from the ballpark to the motel. The KKK never caused us any problems, but we did know that they were at the ballgames. We know that other teams never had issues with them either. Even though their hatred for the Negroes was second to none, we found that the police gave the teams more trouble and more harassment than the Klan. The filling stations and diners also gave us a very hard time. We could pump gas and pay them to fill our tour bus, but we were never allowed to use the bathroom facilities.

I frequently recall when I was in Greensboro, North Carolina during the protest when the kids were in the desegregation demonstration at the drug store and soda shop downtown. The civil rights movement was alive and kicking with bomb threats, people being arrested and stores and restaurants closing in fear of protests and police trying to quell the actions. Knowing the danger that was ensuing and that my life was jeopardy, the New York Yankees called me and transferred me to St. Petersburg, Florida. I had a contract for North Carolina, but they did not want to compromise my safety in North Carolina.

Buried in the quicksand of ignorance, our teams did have hecklers and white people yelling out profanities as we played. We also played games at night until we couldn't see much any more. I recall one game in Norton, North Dakota where a white guy stood in the rear of his pick up truck out by centerfield and called us every kind of cussing and "N-word" in the book. He turned his truck around and just blinded us as we tried to bat and pitch. The North Dakota police finally came by, and told him to leave the area immediately.

We played another game in Nebraska where there was yet another racial incident with white players from the competing team. A pitcher and a catcher came out on the field after putting some mud on their hands, arms and face and Satch told the umpire, "Make them take that off or we're going to leave!" In other places, we had bigoted white folk yelling comments from the stands as we played such as: "Hey! Amos and Andy, turn on the lights, its dark out there!" My manager would yell back to the fans, "Turn the lights on in your bedroom tonight, ya might find me there!" We were not afraid of the people who were yelling all kinds of derogatory remarks at us. They were just being ignorant. We were tolerant of the goings-on at the games and between games.

One of the worst events that I and the team had encountered, took place when the team entertained a large group of women in 1958. One of the women wanted to be with one of the players and did not get her way with him. She got angry, left, and later reported to her husband a much different story. The husband then returned with most of the other spouses. We locked ourselves in where we were staying at the time, which was also one of Ted Rasberry's thirty-nine houses. The players were scared and we began fighting for our lives, defending ourselves as one of the husbands threw a large cinder block and hit me on the back of my left hand. Glass shattered everywhere as I continued on upstairs. I could hear them screaming and yelling profanities at us. I came back down the stairs with a vengeance and pitched the cinder block through the window aiming at the offenders. We heard a blood-curdling scream. We contacted Ted, and he, in turn, contacted the police. The police arrived in minutes and told the perpetrators to leave the area. Of course, Ted was angry, however we, the players, were simply defending ourselves.

In my life and baseball career, the stresses faced were racism, money, overcharging for the ballpark rentals and salaries. By the grace of God, we never got beat up or seriously hurt or even killed…however, it was a little nerve-wracking when we played in an all-white town against an all-whiteteam. Our fears were such that if we won, some of the white guys might get angry and try to beat us up. However, this never happened, and we are all glad of that.

We did have one fight though, to speak of. We had beat Pennsylvania 13:1 and we were in front of the hotel. There were two white men who were circling the hotel five or six times yelling out obscenities at us. Our catcher Ira McKnight said to them, "Pull over!" We were in our pickup truck coming back from a game. We walked over and faced the white folks as they continued to yell at us shouting, "niggers!" Ira said, "Why do you call us these names?" The white leader said, "I'll call you that again!" Ira hit him and knocked him out. Then our pitcher quickly turned around and hit another guy. Another white guy tried to attack me by the truck door. I quickly slammed the truck door on the white guy's hand and broke his fingers. The police finally came after a lot of screaming and name-calling. I informed the police about what had happened and the police asked the white instigators to leave without further provocation.

Much like me, Ira played his first season in the Negro Leagues in 1952 as a fifteen-year old boy. Ira had also lost his chance to play in the Major Leagues. He was catching in the New York Yankee's farm system and already facing a lot of adversity, at the time Yogi Bera and Elston Howard were handling the pitching staff for the big league. During one of Ira's games, he was hit in the hand by a bat. The injury led to his release by the New York Yankee's. He said that the release might have happened anyway; it seemed odd to Ira that he was released after hitting .315, on average that many modern day catchers would love to hit even in the minors. Ira played with us in the Monarchs and in 1963 on the Satchel Paige All-Star teams. After he put down his catcher's glove, he always proudly showed his hands and smiled. How can men such as this continue to smile when their dream was stolen from them? Well, they smile even if they didn't make it to the majors. They got to play baseball and played with and against some great players and they wouldn't trade it for anything.

I recall one evening when were with the Detroit Stars, we got into a fight in Mississippi with black folks because we beat the local black team 19–0 and *boy—they were angry!* My manager, Ed Steele hit the instigator across his lower back with a fungo bat. But our manager ended that fight rather quickly.

There was another disturbing event, as I recall, at a restaurant in Ohio. I recall a white man standing near the counter. The counter top was made of stainless steel. He ordered a slice of pie, as some of our team was sitting at a table in the corner. Two more ball players came in to sit and join us. He continued to stare at us, took a couple of bites of his pie, took out his wallet and slammed the change down so hard on the counter the change was flying everywhere. As he did this, he yelled at the restaurant manager, "Helen, here's your damned money! I'm not eating with these damned niggers!"

The white man left the restaurant. After we had finished our lunch we began to exit the diner and to our amazement, the man had nailed the door shut from the top so we couldn't leave. Ed Steele was trying to push the door open and he couldn't break it down. However, through the windows, we were able to flag down our bus driver, Max, who came over to the door to help us open the door from the outside. Someone called the police and as they arrived, the white man hid behind the police, so we wouldn't try to go after him after we got out. We all watched the white man walk up the street and we just left the situation alone.

We loved Max! All of us loved Max, our bus driver. I recall one day when he rented a horse, wench and put in a used engine when our bus engine died while we played a game. Max had called someone to bring the engine in a pickup truck and met him at the ballpark to exchange the engines. I sat and watched Max replace an engine one day in Satchel's Ford station wagon—it took him no time at all. But all the bus drivers for the Negro leagues were great mechanics. We never had an accident with Max because he was always extra careful of his cargo.

I was in the hotel in Ohio at one point. The hotel's day manager had checked us in. I was sitting in the lobby writing a letter to my family in Virginia. The white folks walked by and stared as if they had never seen a black person write with a pen and paper. I could hear the manager talking to someone on the phone, "We've got a ballclub staying here. The Satchel Paige All-Stars. Them damn niggers have got to go. They can't stay here!" We packed up the next morning and left town. The 'nigger' word floated down through the grandstands almost every time we played, and we did our best to ignore it and just play our best through the shouting and name calling.

On another tour, we were so hungry from riding, and we had just been refused to be served in a restaurant on the road from the night before and had been riding all night from Saxton, Missouri to Lima, Ohio. We were running out of bologna, bread and cheese. We were hard-nosed; whites had much trouble with us eating in the restaurants, but not all of the restaurants. Bologna, bread and cheese consisted of our basic daily diet for a grand total of $2.00 a day. Most times we would pool our money and get a pound of bologna, a pound of cheese and a loaf of sliced bread to split the sandwiches.

The food got a little better as we progressed, but there was some black as well as white resentment that grew. There were times when we entered a white restaurant, only if there were little to no patrons present. The proprietor would give us 20 minutes to eat and get out. These meals were a little better than bologna, consisting of possibly chicken, collard greens, and milk. There were also times in cafes where we could see the white proprietor peeking through the serving glass to see if we were fed up with waiting to be served. These types typically didn't serve us, so we were forced to leave with no meal.

We never knew what we were going to face when we arrived at a food destination, whether we would get served or not. Our bus driver, Max would tell us, "Just take your shaving kit and leave your luggage on the bus because we don't know if the hotel will let us stay." We received a little more respect than the average black individual did, especially if we arrived in our uniforms.

There were times when the police would bring the German Shepherd dogs through the hotel to check on us and in turn, check in each room that we were rooming in. We would show them our uniforms hanging on a hook in each of our rooms. As much as they hated us, it was somewhat hypocritical that we were treated a little better than other regular black people were. I recall another time checking into a hotel, the day before a big game. We were all tired and hungry from the day's travel as we headed to our shared rooms. I had to sleep in the same bed with not one, but two teammates with a bed held up by cinder blocks. We knew we couldn't do any better, but we were happy and proud to continue our games and tours-no matter how difficult the stops were.

The restaurant patrons would wait in their cars or outside until we were done. They would continue to peek in the small windows to see if we were still eating. Only until we left and were down the road kicking up dust, did the white folks bring themselves into the restaurant where we had just been allowed to eat.

We stopped in to play in Saxton, Missouri where we walloped the other team 16–0. When we returned to the hotel, they refused to let us in. The restaurants were all closed to us as well. So we had to jump back in the bus and drive all the way back to Lima, Ohio.

Some of the boys gave in to the temptations of the flesh, but most of them walked away because they knew that venereal diseases were a common place in some of the brothels. This is no different from military personnel, or roadies/music roadies that lived their lives on the road with some of them leaving their families behind. It truly was a lonely ride almost each time for all of them.

I asked Ted Raspberry and the players, "Why do so many women cluster around the players in all the towns, cities and hotels?" I was young. The lesson I learned that day was harsh and well beyond my comprehension, but that scenario continued and I moved forward with my eyes and ears open after that day. They were white women and black women who only wanted to have sex. They weren't interested in money or even getting pregnant. Many of the women were wealthy and some in low and middle incomes, but it didn't matter because both sexes were in it for the sex game. The men paid for sex in the south, but not as much in the northern part of the States and rarely in Canada. Some of the women would follow the players for a hundred to several hundred miles to watch them play and sleep with the players again. Maybe it was because we were like celebrities of the time. Maybe it was a perception that we made good money. We were young, virile men, most of us un-attached. Maybe it was for all these reasons. What was the allure?

None of the players ever stayed behind to stay with the women, this was far too dangerous for any of us. Although, there were several taken by the Canadians for their teams. Their sole motivation was to have sex with the players and sleep with them, of course there was no money to be had to begin with.

This was an age before the sexual revolution, it was all about the perceived money. Although we had a little more money than most blacks, there was fame, there was reporters. Many women believed we had a lot of money because we had little to no expenses; being typically with no family to support, apartment and vehicles. Little did they know that we didn't make that much money after all. Even after a drink or two or a meal at the local night club—the wallets posed a false conclusion.

Most of the time, we drove through an extremely terrifying, segregated and dangerous United States. As we rode on our bus, we would see so many automobile accidents because we were on the rode almost all the time. Sometimes we would be witnesses to these horrible and traumatic events and sometimes they were directed against blacks, and yet, we kept up with the schedule for the next game. I remember driving just outside of Kinston, North Carolina when we came across a car where the front end looked like it was cut off. We saw four black people lying on the side of the road bleeding and broken, so we pulled over and rushed off the bus to help them. One of our teammates ran to the closest house that was several blocks away to have them call an ambulance. We stayed until help came and tried to make them as comfortable as we could. Although the racist, traumatic events happened all the time, it was nothing new and became a way of dealing with life. I believe that, by the grace of God, we stayed safe, and no one was ever really hurt.

Life After Death — General Electric and My Sanctuary

I met my bride, Mary, during high school. She went to Addison and I went to Carver. I had met her at a car show. We dated for a couple of years and I finally asked her to marry me. We were happily married in 1962. She loved baseball as well as attended some of my games.

In 1957, I worked for Walker Foundry, that made brake shoes for trains. I always looked for hard, physical jobs to build muscle. These brake shoes were about three feet long and weighed about seventy-five pounds. When they came out of the molds, they needed to be broken loose with a sledgehammer and put into a large and deep container. It would leave a large burr. I had to lift them out and put them on a grinding wheel to knock off the burr. This was my workout, and on my breaks I would also do fingertip pushups.

This was hard work back then. I had sturdy muscles but I also loved the hard work. When I went to spring training I was in great shape. My kids never got to see me play because we were typically on bus trips to and from games, and there was no room for them anywhere.

Five children later, my beloved wife Mary was pretty much on her own raising the kids. I would come home to work in the wintertime in the off-seasons. Even the guys in the major leagues had to take jobs in the winter time to make ends meet. Many of the guys had to do some barnstorming. Willie Mays, Frank Robinson, Hank Aaron, and Elston Howard got together and did their own barnstorming tours. They were only making less than $30,000.00 a year, but we also had no retirement accounts or pensions to fall back on as most people do today.

I took another job in a produce company and a carpet manufacturing plant rolling up raw wool. My job was to roll up large bolls of raw wool with sheep feces still within the material. We did not have gloves to handle this material and the company surely did not provide them for the laborers. This was the type of job I had during the off-seasons, to keep my family fed and sheltered. My barnstorming days with Satch, were over. Beneath the dust of defeat and the harvest of my regrets—I kept on.

I later drove a produce truck in Roanoke and in the meantime, I put my application in at the end of 1964 with General Electric. One day, a guy who was from India was working in the produce lines as one of the supervisors. A cobra had crawled up into the boxes, climbed out, slithered across the produce floor and cocked his head up high to look at us. The employees went absolutely crazy. We had never heard such a racket with chairs and sticks trying to kill this snake. Some of the people ran out of the building screaming and yelling. I gave it back to the Hindu with my sympathies.

At the end of 1964, I chose to put down my baseball glove and retire my Satchel Paige All-Star uniform for a job as a wireman with General Electric (GE) in Salem, Virginia.

I was bucking for a promotion at GE and I was still in my entry-level job. I talked to one of the foremen about it. What I wanted was a job with more pay. It was a union environment and the white workers predominantly got the jobs before the black people. He saw to it that I got it, I will never know how he pulled it off, but he did and I was happy for that. They had sent the white folks to school and paid for it, but refused to send the blacks. The union really did not represent the entire membership—it was highly convoluted. The whites were promoted into higher paying jobs; they ending up in the union offices without education or training. It was hell at the time. Although, today by comparison, I feel much better about the unions. They take care of their people.

I had a steady job at General Electric in Salem, Virginia, but this was a dark time for my family as I led the charge into a bottle of liquor and didn't come out for almost twenty years. I was still very disturbed and angry from my experience with the Yankees and harbored a deep and brooding resentment. We were paid on Thursday night and I and a couple of buddies proceeded to the bootlegger's where we would cash our checks and stay drunk all weekend. We would go to two or three different unlicensed bootleggers who would acquire ABC legal whiskey and sell it to us with no license.

I always tried to stay away from conflict and was always watching what I said, especially when I started drinking. I do believe that Jekyll and Hyde had made their appearance within me during my drinking years. But, overall, I never wanted to hurt anyone's feelings. I had totally collapsed into a dreary and uncontrollable depression.

My sister Pat also worked at GE for a period of time. I always made her laugh—even today, when we reminisce of the time we worked at GE. Although we worked in separate areas of the factory, we were both wiremen. Pat tells the story of times where I would have an entourage following me on the factory floor over to Pat's desk at her cubicle. The group would then say, "Hey Larry, sing like your friend Charley Pride!" I would start singing, "You gotta kiss an angel good morning, and love her like the devil when ya git back home." But most times, Pat would work the morning shift, and I would work the night shift. There were occasions when a powerful agitation oppressed me and my foreman would ask Pat to take me home because I was so drunk.

I was hung-over on Friday and sometimes missed work on Mondays and Tuesdays. Although this went on for years, alcoholism got the best and the worst of me. I fell prey to disturbing and virulent skirmishes in my head. This went on for years and years with monotonous days of misery and discontent. I was so mad at the Yankees for cutting me, especially after what I did for the Florida League. I was so angry I didn't watch baseball or TV. I stayed busy drinking my liquor, going to jail for drinking and driving and downing a fifth of vodka like it was water—on the job.

GE at one time had 2800 employees at our factory, it was very much like a little community. You could buy your liquor right there in parking lot and pick out what you wanted; drinking and driving was not against the law. It was generally accepted as long as we didn't bring the contraband into the building. Time after time, I had orders to report to the management office and was kicked out of the GE plant twenty-one times for being under the influence of this deep, dark, all-consuming glass bottle. However, GE was known for supporting civil rights in the 1950's through the 1960's as well as social community programs and some funding for minority education for employees and their families.

I remember one evening I was working second shift (3 p.m.-11 p.m.) as I stood at my work area for over twenty minutes I was looking for my missing time card and started to explode with frustration. Unable to locate the this precious card, I went into a sudden burst of anger. In my anger, I threw a temper tantrum like no one had seen—yelling, cussing and throwing anything that was near me, all over a little incident—moments later I found myself at home. Following this eruption, a couple days later, I received a letter warning me not to come back to work. This time I got scared, since I had four children by this time, one of which had epilepsy and my wife to care for. I wondered if they would fire me at my age, I could never find another job such as this one with insurance coverage for myself and my family. This event was an eye-opener showing me the light at the bottom of the bottle. When I returned to beg for my job reinstatement, they summoned me to the senior manager's office. He proceeded to inform me that "*I had a problem*". The penance was to stay home and dry out for three weeks with no pay. When I returned this time—I had an incentive to do my job and with vigor. Evidently, I needed some help for a severe case of depression rather than just case of recreational drinking.

The most difficult working relationship I ever had in my life was during my tenure at GE. I had become a heavy drinker. I remember being drunk as a skunk one day at work and my foreman approached me and said, "Larry, my son wants to play little league baseball and he can't hit a lick. I need you to help show him and teach him". So, the following day, they were with me in the backyard of the plant. I looked around and found a stick, and showed him how to hold a bat, and showed his son that he was holding the bat wrong and had no control. I told the boy that, "You need to be just like Hank Aaron and Ernie Banks—they had quick wrists!" Then I told his dad, "Have your son hold the bat in a finger grip and use his wrists!"

Later on in the year, my foreman proudly brought me a newspaper clipping of his son that had done so well in all his baseball games—he had become a pretty good hitter. My foreman said, "Hey Larry, I've got a pint in the back of my truck for you. Just take my keys and put the keys under the floor mat when you're done with your short drive. Now don't you drink this in the parking lot!" This happened on the job more often than not and once in a while, I would get into some trouble, but things worked out each and every time.

The GE career was my time for alcohol every day on the job and off the job. I was very angry and embittered with the New York Yankees for releasing me, how they did it, and not ever knowing the why's and wherefore's. I had no closure in my baseball career.

I loved to hunt and fish, and belonged to a hunting club in the eastern part of Virginia in Surry County. I went there with my father and brother when I was younger and in my adulthood, the memories would always flood back to me. We met there for deer hunting and fishing.

My father had a camper that sat on a pickup truck. Dusk fell on us and it was time to come home, but before we left, I bought a pint of moonshine at the hunting lodge. I was drinking straight from the bottle in the camper and by this time I was so drunk, I could hardly see straight. The only thing I can remember is that I stepped out...and bounced and dragged on the open highway for a good couple of miles hanging on to the bottom stair rung. A state police trooper pulled along side my father and said, "Stop! You're dragging someone back there!" When Dad finally slowed down, I let go of the stair rung, rolled off the street and ended up on someone's lawn. My face skinned up, all of my clothes were shredded. My daddy, who was half-white and half-black—turned red with anger. The police took me away to jail. Dad made his way to my house and walked in to see my wife Mary and said, "Mary, Lord have mercy that boy needs help!" I was released a day later with my long underwear sticking out in tatters through my pants and with my sweater looking like woolen Swiss cheese. Twenty years after that event, Dad would say, "Shut up! I don't even want to hear about it again!" However, even after this event, I continued to drink. On two different occasions, I had lost my driver's license for a total of three years and many times, I would have to rely on others to bring me back and forth to work. Many of them were people that were unreliable and would not collect me for work and so I'd have to find other ways to get to my job, many times showing up late—it was a humiliating experience for the longest time.

Then came the day, I had to face the music in the manager's office at GE. The hiring/firing manager was present in the room; my shop steward from second shift was there as well. I had just finished a couple pints of vodka mixed with orange juice and concocted a dozen large screwdrivers. My boss stopped at the machine and bought me some mints and said, "Sit as far away from the firing manager as you can." He said, "Mr. LeGrande, you're a great worker with a good continuous record". I said, "Of all the people who have drug or alcohol problems, I surely do not have a problem". He said, "I'm going to do you a favor, I'm going to terminate you—**today**."

Now! I am thinking of my family, my retirement check and my twenty years in service. My steward said, "Let's talk out of the room for a minute." When we returned, he said, "You've got a choice, we'll fly you to Arizona, OR you can attend outpatient detox at the hospital in Virginia and every Tuesday night, you'll have to come here at the AA meetings and other local meetings." I agreed to the last option to go to the AA meetings. The rumor spread that I was to be fired and spread quickly because it was a rare occurrence in those days for folks to get sacked. Several months went by after my AA meetings. The employees greeted me and said, "Hey, can I talk to you about a few things?" I replied, "Sure you can, anytime." As I talked with them, all the men as well as the women would smell of liquor. I knew the problem was much bigger than me. So, I soon became the AA chairman for GE. Most of these people have passed on today and others are quite ill. I drank heavily for over twenty-five years; was it depression? Was it stress? On the other hand, was it anger? Maybe it was all of these. Prior to this, I had been in a daily lifestyle of all that I could drink, eat and rub elbows with famous people in the Negro Leagues.

I only won a prize, one time in my life. It was a case of IW Harper, a $5.00 a ticket raffle at GE. My workmates said to me, "Larry, ya need to get into this raffle". Sid "Army Dog" Watkins, said, "Ahhhh hell no! Give Larry the money and not the liquor!" Well, I ended up winning the case! *Me! Of all people.* I proudly walked out with the case of IW Harper in the parking lot. Everyone was wide-eyed in amazement, there were twenty-five people waiting for me. They all took some and passed it around. The guard walked by, smiled at us, and let us continue drinking. Racism would always magically disappear when it came to sharing liquor. It was like giving candy to diabetic.

I asked God to take the drink away from my lips. I turned down the Arizona trip and the hospital. I went to the meetings and did well, while my family was very supportive. My wife always said, "You're drinking and you have guns, oh Lord, you're going to kill someone!" I would come home from a drinking binge and take out my guns and start shooting in the back yard or I'd be running the state police off the road. How many narrow escapes did I need for a wake-up call? Too many.

My philosophy on life—or what I would share with the world is: Whatever you do, put God first, never undermine people and don't be overbearing. It's something I learned from my father and will always be with me 'till I die. I believe that God wants us to help each other while we are here. With the help of my faith and my family, I was rehabilitated and restored to dignity.

As parents, we've all heard the frightening words, 'I hope I leave this earth before my children.' This was something that was brought to bear not once, but lightning had struck twice for my wife and me.

My son, Johnny, was in college studying criminology. He had received a scholarship and played basketball for the Golden State summer league. One particular day, he was playing basketball and suddenly, without any warnings, he had a coronary in 1982.

Not two years later, my youngest son, Larry Jr. who took after me—had become very athletic. He wrestled and lifted weights in high school. He also worked third shift when he came of age. One morning in 1984, after he had turned twenty-nine years of age, he went to the fitness center as usual. After his exercise routine he proceeded to the hot tub to relax after this workout. He had a horrific seizure in the hot tub and never made it to the hospital.

My oldest son is still with us, but before reaching his golden years ended up on disability working for the railroad as his grandfather before him. Although I still have my precious son and two daughters Lori and Mary, there's no question that there's a void in my heart forever.

It was about this time yet, another 'bombshell' would plummet into my life.

After I lost my two sons, I had put this burden on my wife, mother and father who were by this time, very worried about me. The worst and most painful experiences I have ever had was when I lost my two boys. To this day, it has affected me deeply. I got through it by talking to God and asking Him to help me through it.

When I talk to young people today that are considering baseball, I tell them the first thing is to stay in school—above all you do! Get a decent education, it's first, and sports are second. Listen to your parents and obey God. By the way, get that slack out of your pants and get a haircut! I've talked to numerous schools and school children about the Negro Leagues and a little of my outlook on life. One day, I was speaking to a fifth grade class and told them as I always do: I would like to read today, as many people do. But I'm suffering with glaucoma and do regret that I wish I could have read much more in my lifetime.

I have many fond memories of my professional baseball career in the Negro Leagues and my best friend, Satchel. But the one thing that bothers me to this day, is that I never got the opportunity to play in the Major Leagues. I'm still very bitter over it all, but I'm alive, fairly healthy and have my family, participate in some baseball memorabilia shows, play a little golf for charity fund-raising and attend church. I continue to do my part so that African American youths won't be denied their opportunity for success. Which is why I share my story and my haunts, but most of all—*how I survived and I make the best of what life has to offer me every day.* I had survived the dog-eat-dog Negro leagues, the non air-conditioned 500-mile bus rides in the extremely hot south and all over the country, the bigoted hotel clerks and diners, and the infamous bologna sandwiches that passed as our pre-game meals for top-flight athletes.

In 2005, I drove to Harrisburg, Pennsylvania to play golf in a fund-raising campaign for a police officer who was killed by bank robbers. My foursome was Mudcat Grant, Pee Wee Jenkins, and Chuck Hinton (who recently passed and had played for the Cleveland Indians). The reunion was bittersweet. Although, they didn't play with Satch, they would constantly pummel me with questions about what it was like to play with him. We were also competing with a huge, local event—Notre Dame was in town to play football, so timing was poor. No one came to our fund-raising event, and the money that was promised us didn't materialize.

During my time at GE, we learned of another assassination that would deeply disturb this country's movement towards racial tensions and hurt our heart and soul. In March of 1968, Dr. Martin Luther King was violently taken away from us at only thirty-nine years old. He died not far from where I had played with the Memphis Red Sox in Tennessee. This sent shockwaves throughout GE and the black community. Employees where very distracted and many had trouble dealing with what happened and why it happened. Many were angry, confused, most of us had cried as we tried to discuss, understand and console one another. This man had given the black people hopefulness and leadership. He was the man who ended the terror in the Deep South of being and living as a black person. The terror was not so much segregation, but the fear of murders because the black people could not fight back, or trying innocent blacks and on some occasions whites for crimes they didn't commit. Dr. King had instilled in us strength and courage, much like Ghandi did in helping us to end our fears.

After thirty-two years in 1996, I retired from GE. I often look back at my days in the Negro Leagues and in amazement, laugh and think, *"I went from a cow pasture to Yankee Stadium."*

I often think to myself, ***What I would have done differently in my life?*** I know now, it would have been—to not smoke or drink. Now in my senior years, I feel I was robbed of friends and family. Alcoholism always starts arguments, fights, hard feelings, auto wrecks, shootings, death and more. Although, there were some people that could take two or three drinks and that is all they had. But, I couldn't do that. The depression, the anger, the resentment, the rejection and the anti-climatic portion of my life simply consumed me like a burning fire until I lost total control of myself. It robbed over twenty years of my life with my family and friends and almost killed me.

The best way I knew to try to balance my latter personal and professional life was to go back to my family values. I'd do it over again, without a second thought. That a black man can survive under any condition—we were all simply grateful to play baseball. I think back now and again to my travels and remember that: All the while we were playing, black women as well as white women bought us drinks in the evenings; sometimes we could see that the white men hated and resented us for these actions. But most of all—playing in front of tens of thousands of people is a feeling like none other.

Over a half century has passed since I was released by the New York Yankees and I've not forgotten how I felt when the club let me go from the minor league affiliate in St. Petersburg. Looking back, after a decade that Jackie Robinson had broken the color line, baseball historians say that many Major League teams still had a quota system that held blacks to a higher standard. I know that racism played a part. I was a couple years too soon into the system. When Jackie broke the color barrier, it became a defining moment in American history, an event in the racial crusade in eliminating racial segregation. I loved reading about him when I was a boy. I felt proud and excited to have him play baseball the way he did with courage.

I remember these days clear as a bell, as it was just yesterday, when my father took me as a boy, on the train to Cincinnati to see the Dodgers play. When they announced Jackie Robinson, thousands stood, screamed and cheered. Jackie pulled off his cap and waved it around at everyone. That day was burned into my memory for my lifetime.

There was a long period of time when I was waiting for George Steinbrenner to call me, but the call never came. But several baseball organizations did call. One of which, in 2000, the Negro League Museum invited me to its legacy ceremony in Kansas City. This was an important memory and event where some of the retirees were joined again to reminisce and be honored.

I believe that there is no such thing as luck; you do not find this word in the Bible. I did take many risks with the white people back in the day, but I also took many with the black folks as well. *If you don't take risks or take a chance, then you're at the risk of not taking a chance.*

In 2002, I was inducted into the Salem-Roanoke Baseball Hall of Fame. The former Los Angeles Dodger's star Maury Wills was the keynote speaker a their annual banquet in the Salem Civic Center. The dinner and induction ceremony was a proud occasion for my wife and me. I was among the inductees with: Berkeley "Berky" Cundiff, Kelvin Bowles, Mitchell Page and Dallas Fisher.

I was 66 years old when the *The Roanoke Times*, interviewed me in 2006, where I stated about the deplorable conditions that we experienced including "the low pay, the sleeping and eating in buses and using the roadside as a restroom because many public accommodations were public to everyone but Negroes in those days". I went on to say that, "When I signed with the Yankees in 1959 at the age of 20…I led the Florida State League in hitting in 1960 before the Yankees cut me to avoid paying me a roster bonus. I'm convinced that racism played a role. The Yankees had a star I black player Elston Howard and didn't want to load up their roster with too many other blacks."[1–2]

In the sports section of the *Press & Sun-Bulletin*, (now known as the *Sun-Bulletin*, a daily newspaper for the Binghamton, New York area), my interview with the paper discussed my baseball days as bittersweet. That "there's one thing about my playing days that still bothers me to this day…I never got the opportunity to play in the major leagues." Also, "indeed life is good for me and now I'm doing my part to ensure that African-American youths around the country won't be denied their opportunities for success."[3]

I enjoy talking to people and especially children interested in baseball. I share the ups and downs, but most of all the fun and certainly what an honor it is to play baseball. When the uniform is on, the team is on and so are you. It's a time to shine and to give it your all for the team and for the game.

In 2005, the International League, Gwinnett Braves from Richmond, Virginia played the Richmond Braves and paid tribute to the players of the Negro Leagues when the Braves hosted the Scranton/Wilkes-Barre Red Barons. The salute to the players and teams of the Negro Leagues was presented by Nationwide Insurance and CBS 6. The former Negro League players Samuel Allen, (Kansas City Monarchs, Memphis Red Sox), Gordon Hopkins (Indianapolis Clowns), Henry Mason (Monarchs), Edward Hudson (Stars, Monarchs) and I (Red Sox, Detroit Stars, and Monarchs), were there to assist and promote the event. They provided an exhibit displaying Negro League Baseball and baseball memorabilia. The Braves and Red Barons donned the throwback Negro League uniforms. What a feeling of deep mutual respect that was instilled in these people in order to create a program such as this!

We need more teams and schools to promote the fantastic memory of the Negro League Baseball players. Teams such as the Charleston River Dogs, a Class A affiliate of the New York Yankees, occasionally pay tribute to the history of the game of baseball by featuring "Negro League Baseball Night", via South Carolina State University. In 2008, on a hot summer day of July 26, the River Dogs played a game against the Hickory Crawdads. The River Dogs have been inducted into the Charleston Baseball Hall of Fame in 2007. What a great time for families to come out and enjoy a game on beautiful summer nights a talk of how the game of Negro Baseball came to be with all of its hardship and glory.

Both teams wore replica jerseys emulating the Negro Baseball Leagues. The Charleston River Dogs also wore the

Newark Eagles and the Crawdads adorned uniforms of the Homestead Grays. There I was among today's generation, a catcher for Hall of Fame pitcher Satchel Paige. It was a glorious evening as I starred along with former pitcher Clifford Layton from the New York Black Yankees at the meet-and-greet for the public, signed autographs and spoke to the teams.

Celebrating Carl Long Day (a former player) John "Buck" O'Neil had invited twenty former Negro League Players at an event in 2005. He was Manager for Kansas City Monarchs and for one of his star players—Ernie Banks. Buck was also the first black coach in the Major Leagues.

Courtesy of Larry LeGrande. Photo of Larry LeGrande and Buck O'Neil

Ernie left the Monarchs and went straight to the Chicago Cubs. He had hit .314 in 10 games in 1953. His first great season in 1955 was knocking in 117 runs and hitting 44 homers, a record for shortstops; five of them with bases loaded, at the time, it was a major-league record. Then in 1971 was elected to the Hall of Fame.

Courtesy of Larry LeGrande. Photo of Larry LeGrande in his Satchel Paige All-Stars uniform and Jim Spencer.

Years later at a charity function, I was sitting and talking with Jim Spencer about the Negro Leagues and my friend, Satchel Paige. We had fun as we recalled the early days of baseball.

In the summer of 2007, the White House requested *my presence.* It was such an honor to be recognized by the nation and the capital of the United States. In this glorious and prestigious event, they recognized me at a Congressional tribute in Washington, D.C., with then, President George W. Bush. The feeling was indescribable. We celebrated one of my heroes—Jackie Robinson and other famous Negro League players.

The photo depicts two teams of grade-school children in their baseball uniforms from Brooklyn, New York and children from Los Angeles, California. They played a one-inning game on the White House lawn. This was a commemoration of Jackie Robinson who had successfully broken the color barrier over sixty years prior. Former President George W. Bush, Don Newcomb, who pitched for the Brooklyn Dodgers and a former Jackie Robinson teammate; Frank Robinson who played for the Cincinnati Reds and against Jackie Robinson; Sam Allen, and Tom LaSorda a former manager for the Dodgers. I had a great connection with the former President George W. Bush because he was part owner of the Texas Rangers. He loved to talk about baseball and so did I!

Courtesy of Larry LeGrande.
Photo of George W. Bush, Little League team and Larry LeGrande

I posed in a very memorable photo op with the former President, George W. Bush. As we stood together, he jokingly said, "It had been a long time in coming." I retorted saying, "Yes, it's been 60 years."

Courtesy of Larry LeGrande. Photo of Larry LeGrande, former President George W. Bush at the White House

*Courtesy of Larry LeGrande. Photo of former First
Lady Laura Bush and Larry LeGrande*

Seated in the mini baseball bleachers and playing field they had created for the children were the aforementioned players along with our wives. In sitting with the former first lady, Laura Bush I asked her if they still had all their head of cattle. She stated they had a 'burn' or lightning strike so they sold off their cattle shortly thereafter. We briefly discussed the horrific Virginia Tech incident and she mentioned she was greatly saddened by the event as am I to this day. It pained her to see college folks under such stresses and threatening actions with weapons being carried into the college environment.

THE WHITE HOUSE
WASHINGTON

August 13, 2007

Dear Larry:

Thank you for joining Laura and me at the White House Tee Ball game commemorating Jackie Robinson's breaking of the color barrier in Major League Baseball. Jackie's accomplishments would not have been possible without the pioneer efforts of you and other Negro League players. Your contributions to the game of baseball stand as a lasting legacy and an inspiration to all.

Thanks as well for the autographed baseball card and the hat. Best wishes.

Sincerely,

George W. Bush

Courtesy of Larry LeGrande. Copy of original Thank You Letter from the White House to Larry LeGrande

A few years back, I was reunited with Frank Robinson. I always talked about my best friend Satch and Frank would tell me how great of a talent he was. Frank was so impressed with my story of playing on the Satchel Paige All-Stars. But most of all the Jackie Robinson game-changer story. Frank was the first man to be voted Triple Crown with Cincinnati Reds and Baltimore in the American League. Frank was one of the greatest hitters that ever played ball. His memory and story can be found in the Hall of Fame in Cooperstown, New York.

Courtesy of Larry LeGrande. Photo of Larry LeGrande and Frank Robinson

Courtesy of Larry LeGrande. Photo of Larry LeGrande and Don Newcomb

Don Newcomb said that, "Today's players would never make the tours that we did and wouldn't last a day in the Negro Leagues." 'Newk' was the only baseball player to have ever won the Rookie of the Year, Cy Young and Most Valuable Player. Newk's career average was .271, nailing 15 home runs as a pinch hitter which is an extreme rarity in baseball.

Don was in the Negro Leagues and started pitching at sixteen years old. Don got twenty homeruns and pitched a double header with no fear. He played with Jackie Robinson's teammate. He also pitched to Roy Campinella. Today's pitchers can't seem to pitch more than six innings before the relief kicks in. We had an intense discussion about outfielders not throwing properly to the bases. Just prior the to little league baseball game at the White House.

In one of the interviews with the *The Roanoke Times* in 2002. They stated, "Congressman, J. C. Watts secured a concurrent resolution (HJ92: Commending Larry LeGrande) in Congress recognizing the teams and players of the Negro Baseball leagues—for their achievements, dedication, sacrifices and contributions to baseball and the nation."[6]

An excerpt from the House Joint Resolution No. 92 states as follows:

> "'WHEREAS, Larry LeGrande, an immensely talented catcher and right fielder, is celebrated as a Negro Leagues Baseball (NLB) Living Legend; and
>
> WHEREAS, born on a small farm on the outskirts of Roanoke on May 25, 1939, Larry LeGrande attended school in Salem and was the youngest of nine children; and…
>
> WHEREAS, as a young player for the local Webster All Stars, Larry LeGrande had designs on making it to the big leagues and when the Memphis Red Sox and the Birmingham Black Barons played a game in Salem, the 14-year-old catcher approached a team scout and asked for a tryout as soon as he completed high school; and…
>
> WHEREAS, Larry LeGrande graced the fields of Memphis in 1957, the Detroit Stars in 1958, the Kansas City Monarchs in 1959 and 1961, and the Satchel Paige All Stars from 1961 to 1963 and was called to play for the Yankees' Major League Baseball (MLB) Florida State League team in 1959; and…
>
> WHEREAS, Larry LeGrande's exciting play in the NLB and MLB delighted fans for many years and he is an inspiration to young players aspiring to the game of baseball; now, therefore, be it

RESOLVED by the House of Delegates, the Senate concurring, That the General Assembly commend Larry LeGrande for his athletic ability, and as an exemplary role model for young people throughout the Commonwealth; and, be it

RESOLVED FURTHER, That the Clerk of the House of Delegates prepare a copy of this resolution for presentation to Larry LeGrande as an expression of the General Assembly's gratitude for the baseball memories he afforded baseball fans during the course of his exceptional career.'"[7]

Congressman Watts gathered the former representatives of the Negro Leagues for a small reunion. One of my dreams was to meet Johnny Cochran, my dream came true—there he was at our banquet in Washington, D.C. But this is a discussion for later in my chapters.

I believe it's important to keep this legacy alive and going for generations to come. We were forty in attendance from the Negro Leagues and it was one of the happiest times of my life. I had no idea this kind of thing would be an event of this magnitude and graciousness; I was overjoyed at the opportunity to be there. The renaissance has helped to ease the bitterness because I could not watch baseball for over twenty-five years. I despised it because the Yankees had raw-dealed me. Now I can't seem to pull myself away from watching a game since these events started. Overall, I hit over .300 three consecutive years (1957–1959), led the Negro Leagues in outfield assists (1958–1959), ended up playing with the Satchel Paige All-Stars, my average was .300-plus and I possessed one of the most accurate throwing arms in Negro baseball history.

The News and Observer from Raleigh, North Carolina in 2007 stated, "It has left him (Larry LeGrande) in fine shape for his retirement years. But still, he worries about his old teammates. So he swallows his pride and kindly explains to strangers at memorabilia shows why he and the Negro Leagues mattered."[8]

In my life, the greatest satisfaction these days, is that the good Lord lets me live through my alcoholism abuse. I have my dear friends, and I love God above all. If I were to change things in my entire life, I would wish that I never drank and turned away about twenty years of my life.

Find a Hero or a Mentor—
Find the Trust

Family and friends influenced me in my career in baseball and friendship in my adulthood within General Electric.

I knew how to play pro ball by the time I went to Memphis in 1957 and hadn't yet graduated from High School. I never played little league baseball because it was for the whites only. Some of my best memories were when I had played in the front yard with my brother Doug. He was one of those rare lefties and this is how I learned to hit against left-handed pitching. He pushed me to practice and hone my skills. This was my initiation and to this day I'm thankful to him.

I owe a debt of gratitude to my childhood friends: Arthur Beckley, Jr. who taught me the finer points how to play baseball. Robert "Genie" Simmons, Billy Grafley, Bobbie Barnett, and Richard Hilton. Richard was like a father figure to me. The

Grafleys, our next door neighbors who let us use their field to play. All of whom from Roanoke, were important people in my life because they had believed in my abilities and they would take me back and forth to practice; they were all my role models. They had observed time after time that I never did get out of line and they helped and guided me to maturity.

My high school football coach, Irving Kennedy, Jr. was a huge influence on my life and optimized my skills and schedules. However, my parents would give me a good 'butt-whippin' if I went to play practice before I did my work. I had to clean the chicken house and the hog pen and work the rows of potatoes and beans before I went to practice. These people recognized my talent and continued from the time I was fourteen years old through several years thereafter. I played with friends like Richard Hilton who was forty-two at the time and several others who were much older and bigger than I was.

Courtesy of Larry LeGrande. Larry LeGrande
as a little boy playing baseball.

Arthur Beckley Jr. saw me play and was amazed at what he saw. Usually left-handed hitters don't hit left-handed pitchers because they don't see them as often as they do right-handers. You have a tendency to "look out the window", and pull in the right foot, what we called "stepping in the bucket". The main thing a left-handed batter has to do is to stay in the batter's box. I saw this in today's major leagues—it's a mess the way they reach unnecessarily.

Satch, who was my best friend for the longest time was someone who trusted me implicitly and I certainly trusted him—not only personally, but professionally. It was an education being around him all the time. With his experiences, on and off the field he was more than a mentor to me. Trust is something that never comes easy, but Satch knew I'd never ever betray his trust because I always had the greatest respect for him. *Trust and respect* are the two most important things money can't buy—you have to earn them both. Satch would talk of me now and again and always told people, "Everything Larry talks to you about me—***Believe it!***" Our friendship ran deep. Despite our age difference, we had so many common interests and values.

My hero was certainly Jackie Robinson. I will never be able to say enough about the courage and strength that this man had to break the color barrier in 1947. I know that he's every former Negro Leagues' players' hero in their book. He left a legacy in every players mind and heart that the human spirit is greater than any consternation that is put forth. Without distraction or fear, Robinson would put everyone in awe and amazement with his bravery and fortitude.

My wife Mary, is my angel from heaven. She kept our children and raised them with all of her heart and soul. She's been a tremendous support to me, a great wife, mother and grandmother. For this, I'm eternally grateful for all that she's done for our family. Her moral fabric and her deep, undying, spiritual faith has always kept our family together in good times and in times of adversity.

My sister, Pat, who's ten years older than I, enjoyed watching Doug and I play in the field on our farm. She always got a kick out my sense of humor and dogged determination in my daily life and in our work life together at GE to this very day.

[Interview with Pat, Larry's sister]: "They would play using a broomstick as a bat. If they were lucky, they would find a tennis ball to hit. I remember my mother making dozens of balls for us to play with. She would take pieces of rubber from inner tube tires. Back in the day, the tires had inner-tubes. She would then take the twine from feed sacks we had for the animals. Then take the twine and wrap it around the rubber a hundred times, place it in a sock and made a ball. Doug and Larry played in the field that was cut with a scythe and they would trample down the grass to play and run in the field as they played their baseball games. We always had food, the farm consisted of pigs, chickens, cows, a horse and a goat. We didn't have much time to play, because we always were working on the farm."

Pat and I were always close, she's always said that I made her laugh. We were in Carver School at the same time. It was a sad day, when she moved away from me in Virginia to North Carolina, but I knew we all had to grow up and get married at some point. Pat is and was always someone I could confide in and lean on when times got really rough—my big sister was always there for me.

[Interview with Pat]: "I would be up on the second floor and Larry would be on the first floor. Larry would always try to find me to see what I had whether it was cookies or candy.

He would tell the teachers, "I wanna see my sister!" He was always looking for me. The teachers loved Larry in school, he had a way to make everyone laugh."

But college was not in my long-term plan as it was for all my siblings.

What motivates me today is that I still have a wonderful wife, children, and grandchildren that need me for things now and again. People may call on me for something, my teammates and co-players, still with us, call me almost every day.

The key ingredients to my life have been my integrity. If you promise someone something, do it. This makes for successful relationships. People come to know you by what you do for them. I have over several hundred letters and cards. People will send me my own pictures to autograph.

During my tenure at GE, one of my co-workers, who was having marital trouble took me aside and said, "Larry, I really need to talk to you." He said, "Come with me to the parking lot". He had some free drinks and he was telling me about all his problems. He was white, and he told me that his wife was gone all the time. He asked and pleaded with me not to say anything to anyone. I said to him, "This is very personal, you ask me not to speak about this to anyone—and I will not". I never did speak about the story. But he admired me for respecting his secrets. No one ever challenged me on any of the secrets that I had held for anyone. No one has ever questioned me on my ethics or my behavior.

I was roommate and teammate to Joe Henry, the Clown Prince of Baseball. As I recall, there was a particular young man who wanted autographs. Joe said, "Larry take a chance on this one, and sign it." So, I signed it, Joe Henry gave me the young man's phone number. A young man from Nebraska, creative enough to honor some of the Negro league ballplayers, made baseball cards for me and some of my friends. I've been grateful for this next step into forgiveness and a removal of my bitterness so I was happy to take one more chance. I used them much like business cards in my retirement as I participated in charity fund-raising and baseball memorabilia events in the region for a little extra money to supplement my paltry social security.

There was a moment when thought I had a positive influence on my cousin, Billy Sample from the Texas Rangers. Billy, born and raised in Roanoke, Virginia, played for the Rangers for about five years until he was harassed out of his neighborhood and out of the state. The whites were hanging signs out in front of his house and nooses threatening to hang him if he didn't leave the area. He then went to play for the Braves. I influenced Billy to play for the Atlanta Braves and the Yankees. I attended his mother's funeral recently, and as he approached me, he said, "Larry, you were my biggest influence and talked me into a career in baseball!" Then he said to me, "Larry, you're *MY* hero". I was thrilled to be someone's hero. This made my day—and then some; I always knew he would be good at what he did.

Deception, Equivocation
and a List

Bud Selig, the baseball commissioner appeared on cable TV on CNN announcing the fact that Negro League veteran players would finally receive a portion of the Negro Baseball League Fund. Only some of the players got their portion and approximately forty players did not receive any at all and were never contacted. Bob Mitchell, player for the Kansas City Monarchs, had given a list to the Baseball Commission with these names left off the list. It would appear that when they found that the names were missing they made up the rules after the fact. Some of these Negro baseball players never kept their paperwork to hand into the commission when they requested it and some never had it to begin with. My friend, Charley Pride, a multi-millionaire, modestly told them he did not need the money and to give to those who are in desperate need. However, he was given the funds in spite of his plea. So he took his portion and gave it to his brother.

I had called Jim Martin and sent him documentation with my social security tax forms and where and when I had played on the Negro Leagues. By then, they said, "It was too late and they had doled out the money." I was in Washington at one point regarding the Negro Leagues resolution. Johnny Cochran was in attendance. When I informed him of this disgraceful act, he was outraged. Joe Henry wrote to Bud Selig after the fact and he got his check for $33,033.33. Buck O'Neil had already become a millionaire, so he didn't care much about the fund and did not care to take the time to help us get any funding to help the needy.

Courtesy of Larry LeGrande. Photo of Larry LeGrande and Johnny Cochran.

To this day, I believe that some of these black folks resent each other so much they cannot lift a hand to help each other. Now, there less than a couple dozen of us left most living in poverty level or in nursing homes; so it would not be a stretch, for the MLB to pitch in and help the people who were icons of their game.

A half a century later in 2004, Major League Baseball, namely Bud Selig, announced that they would provide over $1 million dollars in pensions to former Negro League players in their new charitable program.

The *Associated Press* from New York published the following: "Major League Baseball will provide more than $1 million in pensions to former Negro Leagues players through a new charitable program. The fund will benefit 27 players, all of whom played after Jackie Robinson broke baseball's color barrier in 1947.

"I am pleased that we are able to come to the aid of former Negro League players who are in need," Commissioner Bud Selig said Monday in a statement. Major League Baseball and the Baseball Assistance Team will handle the program. Baseball set up a program in 1997 to provide pensions to Negro Leagues players before 1948. The new fund will benefit additional players who spent parts of at least four seasons in the Negro Leagues, starting before 1958.

The agreement was first reported by The Washington Post. Players will have the option of getting $833.33 per month for four years—a rate of $10,000.00 per year—or $375.00 a month for life. 'That's great. Good for them,' said former Negro Leagues player Buck O'Neil, chairman of the Negro Leagues museum in Kansas City. 'They deserved to get something.'

In March, Selig told Sen. Bill Nelson, D-Fla., that a proposal would be made to cover players left out of a Negro Leagues pension fund created in 1997. That agreement set up annual pensions of $7,500.00 to $10,000.00 for players who spent a total of four years in the majors or Negro Leagues, including at least one day in the big leagues, after 1947.

The players affected by the new agreement did not play in the majors. Nelson had said these players did not get a full chance to make it because, even after Robinson joined the Brooklyn Dodgers, not every team was integrated until the Boston Red Sox became the last club with a black player in 1959. 'Not every team thought it needed a black ballplayer right away,' O'Neil said. 'The New York Yankees didn't until they got Elston Howard. The Red Sox didn't, either.'

A list of 27 was given to the MLB to help retired Negro League Baseball players. "Bud Selig told Sen. Bill Nelson, D-Fla., that a proposal would be made to cover players left out of a Negro Leagues pension fund created in 1997. That agreement set up annual pensions of $7,500 to $10,000 for players who spent a total of four years in the majors or Negro Leagues, including at least one day in the big leagues, after 1947."[29]

The list was not comprehensive, and not only left out several of the players, but when MLB distributed the fund the backlash provided an interesting insight: Some of these players didn't play in the majors. Some didn't get a full chance to make it because after Robinson joined the Brooklyn Dodgers, not every team was integrated until the Boston Red Sox became the last club with a black player in 1959. The New York Yankees didn't until they got Elston Howard in 1955.

My friend, Joe Henry had written a letter to Bud Selig, the Commissioner of Baseball and also sent a copy to the Negro League Baseball Museum saying, "after contacting your office and being told I was required to submit an application—which I did—I eventually received a rejection response concerning the personal information I disclosed in my application that left me completely in dismay. It is hard to reconcile how MLB, an organization that Negro Leaguers pointed in the right direction of becoming Major League caliber after entry, would belittle itself by hoodwinking the American public by using electronic and print media to convey how "benevolent" it presently is towards the former Negro Leaguers, following the destruction of this once powerful economy within the Black community. Joe went on to say, "As a former Negro Leaguer—having begun my career in 1950 with the Memphis Red Sox...I am appalled by the lie of questioning found in the application I received, which was regarded as "Grant Application" of which I supposed is tantamount to that designed for an ex-convict." Joe further reiterated the announcement, "according to Selig in the newspaper article, the new fund would benefit players who spent *"parts of at least four seasons in the negro Leagues"*, which automatically made me eligible." Joe said, "as far as I'm concerned—it smells of a scam." Joe further stated, "In the year 2000, following dissipation of the initial amount of money, which took place in approximately three additional checks, I—like numerous former Negro Leaguers—received a last check from MLBP amounting to $3.26. This embarrassing "donation" by MLBP motivated me to cast it aside as useless, only to reactivate it following recent disapproval of my application." Joe stated his ailments and physical challenges and mentioned the Veteran's Administration was assisting with some of his health-related expenses. He then went on to say, "Many former players—who did not receive any of the fund money—having similar problems, were not as fortunate as I, because of not having a military background."

I experienced the same situation with not only Bud Selig, but with the Baseball Assistance Team (BAT) who has contradicted the announcement of the fund and Bud's position in assisting former Negro Baseball players. As Joe further stated in his letter regarding BAT, "However, after adhering to your policy—only to have the application rejected due to being so candid—I became very disgruntled, especially when informed that according to your charter and by-laws, I was outside the perimeter of qualifying for that, which was being offered because my income exceeded my expenses. To make matters worse, it was indicated that a minimum of three years was necessary for me to be eligible. Thus, I found myself in a no-win situation, beginning with our statement regarding the "required" minimum of years. By declaring such provision, you contradicted Selig's position relative to *"parts of at least four years"*. In so doing, I was automatically eliminated. Additionally, Selig—by stating in his press release that the fun would benefit 27 players, who started before 1958—substantiated my no-win situation, because during that year I played for "Goose Tatum's Detroit Clowns" with teammates, such as Art Hamilton and Larry LeGrande, and playing against the likes of Ray Haggins, Charley Pride, the Country Western singer, and others."

In speaking with my friend, Charley Pride who was already a millionaire, he received his payout and didn't need it. He informed me that he gave it to his brother. Some of these instances caused conflict among those who received the payout and those who did not and should have been on the list.

Joe stated he was entitled to $50,000.00, but went on to say in his letter, "Furthermore, it would heal the rift between the 27 players receiving funds and those who have been denied, and—not to omit—by using this method, it would test the sincerity of MLB by wiping the slate clean. In doing so, it could truly be said that MLB is a benevolent donor rather than a pretentious deceiver."[30]

My friend, Charles Johnson who was trying to help over 100 former Negro League players accepted into a formal pension fund, passed away in 2006 before he could claim any reward or support checks from the pension.

I love Ted Turner and what did when he brought Satchel Paige to the Atlanta Braves. With this contract, Satch was able to qualify for his MLB pension. This act of bending the rules simply added Satch to their roster, but Satch deserved it and Ted Turner was kind enough to allow this to happen.

I received a similar rejection letter from the BAT stating that I "had one year in the New York Yankees Minor League system." They also made assumptions that I had not played on all these teams. The BAT once again contradicted Bud Selig's terms in saying that, "To qualify the years of service had to be with teams that were eligible to send their players to the annual East-West All-Star Game held at Comiskey Park. In 2004, a new charitable program was created as an addition to the 1997 program and was designed to assist players whose four years of service were achieved after 1948."[31]

"In matters of race, in matters of decency,
baseball should lead the way."

—A. Bartlett Giamatti

In another article written in the *Bleacher Report*, "Four years later, MLB again attempted to correct the injustices of the past by giving 29 veterans of the Negro Leagues life annuity payments worth $7,500.00 to $10,000.00 per year. That same year, the league also bestowed life annuity payments totaling $10,000.00 per year to retired Caucasian men, such as 1941 National League Most Valuable Player

Dolph Camilli, who played prior to the establishment of the players' pension fund in 1947.

Seven years later, in 2004, President Obama's predecessor in Congress, United States Senator Carol Moseley Braun, appealed to Florida Senator Bill Nelson to urge Commissioner Bud Selig to expand that class of retired Negro Leaguers, arguing that baseball wasn't truly integrated until 1959, when the Boston Red Sox added Pumpsie Green to their roster. And sure enough, 89 additional men received new lifetime payments; though the terms were a bit different, each of these Negro Leaguers was promised $40,000.00 for four years, or $350.00 per month for life. And finally, in 2008, acting on a proposal from Hall of Famer Dave Winfield, MLB held a mock draft: in the interests of diversity, each MLB team selected a living veteran of the Negro Leagues and paid him a signing bonus of $10,000.00. Not too shabby, you're probably saying to yourself. Giamatti would be proud.

So all this generosity begets the logical question—if MLB is so intent on doing the right thing for all those men who it didn't have a contractual employment history with, why does it continue to hose all those retired ballplayers who it did have legitimate contractual relationships with? Now if you can answer that, you're smarter than me.

Sure, most of these 900 or so guys are Caucasian, but many of them are persons of color. Take Herb Washington, for instance. The famous designated pinch runner for the Oakland Athletics who Mike Marshall picked off during the 1974 World Series has done alright for himself during his post-baseball career, but that's not the point. He's not getting health insurance coverage from his time in The Show.

Neither are Billy Harrell, of Albany, New York; Aaron Pointer or Louisiana native Wayne Cage. But it's not just

African-Americans who are being hosed by MLB. Neither is a guy like Mexican-American Dick Baney, who played alongside Jim Bouton on that expansion Seattle Pilots team famously chronicled in Ball Four. Or Cuban-American Facundo Antonio "Cuno" Barragan, who caught for the Chicago Cubs. I could go on, but I'm sure you smell what the Rock is cookin'. The only question is, does MLB?"[32]

The Old Virginia
Homestead Estate

Time marched on and before we all knew it, my father was 104 years old and my mother was 100 years of age. The homestead we lived on was a farm also known as Pinkard's Court.

Courtesy of Pat Davis. Photo of former homestead at Pinkard's Court in Roanoke, Virginia.

One morning, they received a letter from a local realtor asking for a portion of their property. They were to build a secondary road that would parallel Route 220. They soon contacted them by phone and Dad said that he didn't want to sell his property. The realtor then sent a follow up letter with a formal offer for his property.

At this time, my father didn't know how much a loaf of bread cost, much less what his property was worth. The cost of living had passed him by years and years before. I had taken him to the VA hospital at one point, and he handed me $5 to get 5 gallons of gas to fill up the gas tank. At that time the gas was over $2.00 a gallon. Dad had retired on disability in 1952; he would receive $512.00 a month for the remainder of his days. As for my mother, her doctor had written us a letter that she was incapable of signing any documents and is not of sound mind due to her deteriorating aging condition.

The realtor returned with yet, a second offer for $212,000.00 for the farm. Dad said, "I'll take that". When I heard of this infringement on my beloved parents, I hired an attorney. Meanwhile, I contracted with an appraiser to evaluate my parents homestead. The property was appraised at $535,000.00. I, in turn, communicated this to a couple of my sisters.

Today, the retail parcels are going for a million for less than two acres of land. The commissioners also stated that the commercial property would be bringing in at least a half million in tax revenues in the first year.

When a couple of my sisters learned of the quick cash, they didn't care for my parents or the appraisal process, but wanted the money for themselves. I was paying for attorney fees and court costs with stock that I was selling from my tenure at GE. My sister Pat helped me with some of the attorney fees and the appraisal for the property. I would have turned the property over after a proper due process and appraisal in all fairness, but this process was far from fair. The attorney never told us during the process of the name of the construction group that was trying to take my parents' property. Judge Apgar was also a long-time friend of my father's at the time. As events progressed, my father turned ill and was flat on his back in the VA hospital. I found myself in the courthouse once again. The judge informed my other sister, Pat who was also local as I, that she would be in contempt of court if she didn't sign the documents turning the estate over to the construction company. The judge had turned the case over to the chancery and appointed Salem attorney Fielding Logan. It was followed two weeks later by a hearing with the attorneys for the construction company, my attorney and a couple of my sisters. Across the room I had glanced at the judge sitting with another representative and the judge stated, "I'm not going to fine Ms. Davis for contempt of court". He went on to say, "I'm going to pass this issue onto the chancellor".

Two weeks following this event, I found myself with my sister, Pat, the attorneys for both sides and the judge at yet another hearing.

Unbeknownst to my poor mother, she had recently signed their papers, and then informed her children that she thought she was going to a nice nursing home. Neither one of my parents were allowed to sign any paperwork. But my sister, who was desperate for cash had them sign over the property. The attorneys acquired a copy of this from the doctors and claimed that the property had been signed over.

The Roanoke Times reported, back in the fall of 2000, "Two of L.S. And Fannie LeGrande's children say developers didn't pay enough when they bought their 4.5-acre Roanoke property. It sits abandoned and practically empty, a broken house with out a family inside." It had been ransacked and looted as well. "But the dilapidated 4.5-acre property, overgrown with grass and weeds, look like a thing of beauty to the Southern Lane Group. The Roanoke developer paid L.S. and Fannie LeGrande $215,500.00 for the land they lived on for more than 75 years in one of the city's oldest predominantly black neighborhoods.

Southern Lane believes it's the last piece in a jigsaw of acreage that will feature restaurants, shops and an 89-room motel.

But the deal, which 104-year-old L.S. LeGrande and his 100-year-old wife, Fannie signed nearly three years ago, is on hold. The family is divided as a legal dispute winds its way through the courts." I knew that the property would be worth millions and my sister Pat and I tried to fight this in court. Because my father didn't know the value of many things at 104 years old, we had the courts and the developers as well as certain individuals in my family working against us to evaluate the property. As we were facing the court battle, my sister Pat who had power of attorney for our mother was facing contempt of court for refusing to sign, even though our mother was documented as being incompetent to sign anything. By this time, I was sixty-one and my sister Pat was almost seventy. The paper went on to say, "Today, Davis faces a contempt of court charge. Roanoke Circuit Court Judge Jonathan Apgar has ordered her to either sign the papers that will close the sale or put up a bond for the sale price until her appeal is decided. Southern Lane argues that she has done neither. Davis' attorney, John Edwards said he will argue that she is not required to.

Logan ruled that the sale would go forward. Fannie LeGrande was competent when she signed the paper, and the house sold for fair market value, he ruled. Apgar upheld all but one of Logan's rulings. Fannie LeGrande's mental condition had, in fact, deteriorated by the time she signed the papers. Apgar ruled. Davis as her guardian would have to sign the papers for her. The rulings made Larry LeGrande bristle. He said he believes his parents were cheated by a conspiracy, and his siblings poorly advised them on the deal. He isn't ready to give in."[27]

In a later article from *The Roanoke Times* said, "In 2002, some Southern Hills residents expressed frustration and concern over how the store might affect their property values and quality of life. They wanted to know what the city was doing to improve the long-term viability of the area.

Residents of the predominately black neighborhood have been feeling the crush of booming development along 220 for years now. A Wal-Mart, Outback Steakhouse and other businesses have popped up, along with residential development at Pheasant Ridge and Southmont." They further stated, "Some residents were outraged to learn their streets would be used for noisy, dust-stirring construction traffic, but then would be closed off from the subdivision after a main gateway opened on Peakwood Drive in South Roanoke."[28]

The next thing we see is mountains of soil piled up on the side of my parents' property and they're excavating the area. I personally didn't want to sell because I still loved farming and wanted to continue to raise cattle and grow a large vegetable garden. Now we see the likes of Chik-fil-A and Home Depot on my parents' land that was once a sprawling homestead and farm.

As tragedy would have it, I lost my brother Doug to lung cancer. We all smoked, it was inevitable and devastating. We all knew it was bad, but we all awaited our summons to our last puff. Doug had mentored me into my life of baseball and I'll always be forever grateful to him.

Some time later a similar situation happened across the street from my parents' homestead. There lived over twenty black families. These were not middle class and certainly were not upperclassmen, but poor and unemployed black people. Each family was offered various amounts from a pool of money. Lowe's had put up over $1.5 million and took their properties and began razing the area in a rapid stream of land clearing.

My sister Pat stated, "It was a surprise to me how things came about in the 1997–1998 timeframe. My father was 104 and my mother was two months short of 102, when they passed. My two sisters were short on cash, so when they got wind that there was an offer on the homestead, they decided to put my parents in a nursing home. They were living out of state, so it came as a shock to me that my father would have them take care of my parents' final affairs. My father had given them power of attorney, even though Larry and I were close by and were fighting to keep the property in-tact. My parents were both senile by this time and I remember my father saying that 'he didn't like this situation, because they made it public.' My father decided he didn't want to stay at the nursing home because he felt he wasn't getting the care he wanted and transferred to the Veterans hospital; leaving my mother alone for the first time in her life.

A powerful agitation and a rush of hatred and loathing came over me as I tried to understand what was happening and why people would undermine two very aged and senile, elderly people such as these.

A Century in Life of a
Loving Couple—Roanoke Icons

My father, L.S. LeGrande was born July 31, 1896 in Richmond County, North Carolina. He attended school and later began his work in 1910 for Taft Lumber. He was also a retired World War I veteran. He married my mother, Fannie LeGrande and moved to Roanoke, Virginia in 1921 were he worked at the Norfolk & Western Railway Freight Station. My mother, was relegated to work as a house cleaner for three dollars a day in a wealthy white Roanoke Virginia country homestead. In 1924, he purchased acreage at Pinkard's Court working a small farm with various farm products. Being a hard-working man, he also painted houses for extra income to provide for his extensive family. He finally retired in 1952 on disability and became a deacon board member of his church where he served his community with great pride. My father passed on October 18, 2000 at the V.A. Medical Center in Salem, Virginia.

My mother, (Fannie LeGrande) was born January 22, 1900 in Rockingham County, Rockingham, North Carolina. She was from a family of nine children, she too went on to have nine children as well. She had a quest for knowledge and believed that much knowledge would be gained through travel. She did get to travel with her free pass with my father's employ at the railroad. Her love of knowledge, adventure and reading inspired all of us, which is why mother didn't particularly hesitate when she received the letter for my request to play for the Monarchs. She loved people and had a sharp wit about her. She would always tell us to 'do the right thing.' She was active in her community and cared about poor people. She was also very involved in the church and had been a member of the original board of directors of Total Action Against Poverty (TAAP); now known as Total Action for Progress (TAP). My mother passed on November 27, 2001 at the nursing home.

Courtesy of Pat Davis. L. S. LeGrande and Fannie LeGrande

Prior to my parents' passing, they would bear the tragic deaths of five of their children, and two of their grandchildren. Their youngest daughter was born in 1945, but only survived for one day. My eldest brother, Spurgeon passed in 1999; he had been ill since he was struck by a car two years prior. He had worked at the railroad after many years of faithful service. My sister Jacquelyn was employed by the local nursing home and had lovingly provided care for the elderly and those confined to convalescent homes. My sister Jacquelyn passed in 1992. As for my dearest brother Doug, I'd been told that I was a lot like my brother in many ways. He loved fishing, hunting, tennis and was truly my mentor and hero. Doug had perfected his mentorship craft at the Warwick State Training School in New York City for boys. He had touched the lives of many boys and put countless individuals back on the right track in life. He guided them in their efforts to be more responsible and compassionate toward their peers and others. My dearest brother Douglas passed in 2000. My sister Jean was a retired veteran of the United States Air Force and later served for the State of New Jersey as a supervisor with a loving heart, for special needs individuals. My sister Jean passed in 2004 at her residence in South Carolina. My other sister Earnestine passed on November 9, 2014. She was eighty-four years old. She had dedicated her life to teaching.

Mom and Dad had been the proud parents of nine children, twenty-six grand children and fourteen great-grand children. My parents were buried along with my baby sister, Karen who only lived for one day. Throughout the century they endured tragedies, death, love, compassion, challenges, hard labor and forceful segregation. Through these people we learn to have resilience, courage and the strength to endure hardships and embittered people as well as the love of family and friends that flock to support us in our times of darkness to bring us light and joy.

It has been almost three decades now that I have been sober, and I am thankful that my parents saw me sober before they passed away. It truly is a horrible and devastating addiction.

It's been said that less fortunate African-Americans of today are at an immense disadvantage. The average family has security, trust, hope, education, counsel, and direction from their parents and siblings that they can trust and lean on as they get older. The disadvantage comes in with lack of education and life coaching for the children and even for the young adults as they progress through life. The culture among the less fortunate and the more fortunate African-American has since widened the gap in the haves and have-nots. My father became extremely protective of his money and personal affairs even in the face of his wife and children. He had to fight for every dollar he earned not only against the whites, but also the blacks back in the day all the way up until the day he passed. As he surpassed being a century old, he could no longer differentiate from the people he could trust and not trust—family or not. I know I have my mother's faith and moral values at my side in matters of the heart and home. Not to say that my father was unethical, but it was all he knew to scratch out a living and protect his family in his time. My mother was a God-fearing woman and although she had lost her mental capabilities at the end of her life of almost a century of hard knocks, she would fail to understand the tragedy that unfolded about their home and the conflict that was brought about by a couple of my financially desperate siblings.

In my discussions by Johnny Cochran, prior to his passing, he was simply outraged at the injustices that were served on my plate. He was anxious to meet with me to right the wrongs and said that he was "So disturbed by what the retired negro fund had done and what the powers-to-be had done to my parents that he was willing to help me pro bono!" But as my fate would have it, we lost Johnny tragically soon after our discussions.

I've made my peace with God and the church, but I still carry a heavy heart for the injustices, lies, corruption and the collusion that I'd seen in the midst of the fight and battles to not only gain justice for myself, but for others' welfare as well.

Afterword

This writing is a labor of love not only for my friend, Larry LeGrande, but for the relationship, the intense bond he had with Satchel, the love of baseball and his resilience to the offenses that they experienced throughout their lives. Try pulling up a chair near a loved one or a friend and ask them to tell you their life story. Listen, understand, learn and ask questions—you'll never know what you'll discover on this kind of fascinating journey.

I wrote his story to not only leave behind his legacy, but it's also a cleansing for his soul. My hope is that we'll find vindication and some redemption in the last few years of his life. I think there's no better exercise for my heart and mind than to reach down and lift people up.

In my absorbing, brief discussions with Satchel's daughter, she once stated, "Many people claimed they knew my father, but Larry was the only one who really knew him." I shared with her my Canadian heritage and of my dad who loved fishing and hunting as well. Also, that I lost my father a month after she lost hers, but the memories linger as we continued to share our bitter-sweet stories.

Have you had a best friend and soul mate that has passed before you? Or a sibling, daughter or son? Have you been the subject of ridicule, anti-Semitism, racism, jealousy, envy? These are all ways of showing scorn for a person or group of people or types of people. Could it be that some people ridicule others because they're envious of others' achievements or they are simply attempting revenge, retribution or rebellion? Many of these Negro League players, when ridiculed, didn't do much to defend themselves as they knew it would give the ridicule vindication. Larry fondly talks of his best friend, Satch to this day. How great are the pale shadows of yesterday of those who smile from some dim corner of our memories!

Perhaps the most single difficulty these players faced in their early years was the perseverance to attain acceptance in the public eye within the racist realm. The Jim Crow era demonstrated cultural and intensive conviction that a particular race had a hereditary superiority over another. This included aggressive, abusive behavior towards members of another race producing feelings of anger or rage. There's a lapse from the human intelligence and decencies of a civilization. Larry is just one example of man's hopes and dreams that were ripped to shreds, until now he's maintained discreet reticence amid his distress and humiliating life events. Larry has suffered and languished in his obscurity, but has risen above and to this man we owe him chivalrous homage of respect. Magnanimity is greatness of the soul and Larry took the flight beyond the reach of his own expectations. He never gave up even in the face of dark dissolutions.

The Negro League players believed they were just as good if not better than some of the Major League players.

In many instances, this proved to be true. Larry was one of those quality players who should have fulfilled his dream and attained Major League status. He was cut from the opportunity to reach the Major Leagues and his cut remained within his soul, that has continued to hemorrhage for over fifty-five years.

Who, if anyone would step up to the plate and clear the injustices that plagued Larry?

Although, he tried with all his heart, mind and soul, he had put forth trust in people who had the power and decision-making capabilities and opened his wallet in a case that was diseased with greed, back-door deals, politics and crooked business men.

Why would an economic development organization undermine the fabric of a family already in turmoil that was facing death and utter despair? The deals had already been locked in years prior to the land development and the families who were victims of the raw deals were simply 'after the fact' and something to push aside in order to achieve their goals. The aging couple, not of sound and mind body were coerced to sign over papers for the sale of their farm and homestead for pennies on a dollar. Further, to take advantage of an very elderly, desperate woman who had become power of attorney for her parents, only within their final days—none of which were of sound mind. What fragment of society would come to bear on weak individuals such as these? I would make the case for human character that the best test of man is power and authority. The real danger are those in authority who deny others' rights and reject accountability and responsibility as they plunder the less fortunate citizens. After all, how can something be politically right if it's morally wrong?

Virginia law has what they call a commissioner in chancery. The commissioner hears evidence and reports back to a judge with a ruling who has the option to overturn the ruling. They had a 102-year old man in hearings and made him take a deposition. Who in good conscience, would engage the very elderly in an unethical legal process or any legal process whatsoever? However, as our days grow darker with greed and power, many of us have seen mediators and individuals such as these that come to the table with their own biases and judgmental pre-conceived notions that should proceed with reasonable diligence, but fail to do so. In Larry's parents' case, the chancery ruled that they were competent to sign papers and the sale would go through. The judge ruled that Larry's mother was not, in fact competent and that the daughter would have to sign over the homestead. If the daughter, namely Pat would not sign, she would be found in contempt of court. The attorney poorly advised the family as well as Larry, the hearings only took a couple of afternoons and Larry's persistence and formal appraisal would go by the wayside in the circuit courthouse.

In Larry's case, I believe that when your anxious about accomplishing something that you feel is right, you forget about fear, you're in the realm of fearlessness. But as he strove through his goals and reached the higher highs the disappointments were lower lows, these of which were disappointments in humanity, and even within his own family. Was he relegated to a time and place? Was he a victim of this circuit court? Was he a victim of his own ethical beliefs, values and morals that he strove to understand? There are African-Americans who are afraid to stand up for their beliefs and rights because they're afraid that something may happen to them. Larry was not afraid to speak his mind and try to stand up for the rights of his family amidst disillusion, confusion and greed. Finally, Larry's very elderly parents and those in authority did have one thing in common—that they cannot always be relied upon.

Being with Larry, he demonstrates a disarming honesty about himself. As I tried to find closure for him in writing to some of these powers-that-be…many of them closed the door, pleaded ignorance and passed the buck. In terms of helping Larry attain his portion of the Retired Negro League Fund, I went insofar as enlisting a local attorney to research and investigate the outcome and program that the MLB had begun for the retired Negro Leaguers. Much to our dismay and shock the attorney's findings and response from the MLB was that it was: "Very political and that we needed to stay far away from this problem." Many of those in power possess an unnatural power that consumes and corrupts the understanding and the heart of their victims.

My husband, Jim attempted to give Larry closure to his fifty-five years of agonizing and obsessing of how he could be cut with all his talent. Jim had a compassionate idea and truly believed that the New York Yankees organization would step up to the plate for a life-changing request on Larry's behalf. In calling the New York Yankees organization headquarters, Jim spoke to several managers to inquire about giving Larry a contract for a day to honor and recognize him for his superior talent in the New York Yankees Minor League system. The New York Yankees organization shut the door again. They said, "They only do that kind of thing for players that were in the Majors." The point is, he was not given the chance to play in the majors because of racially-motivated player personnel decisions in the early 1960s, irregardless of his talent. So wouldn't you think that New York Yankees organization would do *something? Anything at all?* After all, if the White House can honor the Negro League players, why shouldn't the New York Yankees organization? Moreover, in passing the buck, they told Jim to call Cooperstown if we wanted to give Larry recognition. Research shows that the Yankees, do in fact, give short-term honorary contracts to recognize certain individuals such as Billy Crystal, and their HOPE program that recognize individuals or groups of people that have spectacular stories.

One has to wonder, what would the Negro League ballplayers' lives would be like if things were different, if humanity wasn't caught up in the evil age of segregation and steeped racial tension blanketed by oppression. The only way I could offer Larry closure is to write his life story in the hopes that his aspirations, life, accomplishments and disappointments would be shared with the would-be readers. The validation that Larry was as good as Willie Mays…is in and of itself the inspiration of this writing. Larry knew he was good, other key figures did as well. So where did we go wrong with this ballplayer's skill and talent? One will never know the real outcome if he would have *not been cut,* one thing we do know for sure, is that he would become good enough to become one of the Satchel Paige All-Stars.

As we examine the Canadians and baseball, my Dad was in his twenties when he played on the Stella Maris team in Nova Scotia, Canada. The team was part of the Claire League in the Maritimes. The only person still with us is James Ayers (as of this writing). James told me, "Camille was a tremendous pitcher with an extremely strong arm—he was VERY good. He was a very good man too." James had played short stop and still enjoys the game of baseball to this day at ninety-seven years young. He said, "We only got to play about five years or so, then everyone was drafted to the war." Again, one will never know, if fate would have brought them to the Majors. After all, Canada's first MLB team was the Montreal Expos, through rapid league expansion in 1969 teams formed all over Canada and baseball had become very popular since its inception in 1838 in Ontario.

While there's no major leagues in Canada, there's one Major League team—the Toronto Blue Jays of the United States based Major League Baseball. Moreover, the percentage of Major League Baseball players born outside of the United States continues to rise. Further, it must be said, that our own Jackie Robinson was playing for the Montreal Royals of the International League (Brooklyn's Triple A farm team), by Branch Rickey just before he signed him the following year in 1947 to the Brooklyn Dodgers. Jackie Robinson became a beloved figure in the city of Montreal as he led the Royals to the Governor's Cup. In the Ken Burns' documentary film *"Baseball"* the narrator quotes Sam Maltin a stringer for the Pittsburgh Courier: "It was probably the only day in history that a black man ran from a white mob with love instead of lynching on its mind." In Rickey's foresight he wanted to make sure that his eventual signee would be able to withstand the racial abuse, threats and all of the horrors he would face in the Majors.

Photo courtesy of author. Photo of author's dad, Camille Thibodeau (upper right) and James Aymar (upper left) of the Stella Maris Nova Scotia Baseball Team.

My parents, Ann and Joseph Thibodeau were born and raised in Nova Scotia, Canada. Immigrated to Lawrence, Massachusetts by the late 1950's and became citizens of this great country in the latter part of the 1970's. Lawrence was the place where my father met Dom DiMaggio. Dom had recently retired as the long-standing center fielder for the Boston Red Sox, and founded the American Latex Fiber Corporation in the Merrimac River Valley. My father befriended Dom DiMaggio and traded baseball stories.

My father who had become an electrician by trade, assisted Dom in his factory when machines would break down or electrical problems emerged. Dad had been working for some time at Malden Mills in Lawrence, Massachusetts. He was frequently summoned to fix or install electrical items or wiring for Dom, Dad never asked for payment in return.

One day, Dad asked Dom if he knew anyone that was selling their used car. Dom DiMaggio decided that he didn't want one of his old cars any longer and said, "Well, it really wasn't running anyway." And gave it to my father. After a long argument where my father had a great deal of trouble accepting this free gift in return for his years of service, he finally gave in to this gift that was bestowed upon him. Dom said, "It's an old beat up station wagon that needs a lot of work." Dad said, "That's great, my brother-in-law just moved here from Canada and needs it because he's got six kids." They laughed and days later my uncle Donald and Dad were found in the street working on the car, replacing the pistons, a tune-up and giving it an overhaul. Years later, Dad passed suddenly in July of 1982 on his last vacation trip with my mother in Quebec, Canada at the early age of fifty-eight a month after we lost Satchel Paige.

The interview in July of 2014, with Larry LeGrande's sister, Pat, was absolutely enjoyable. Pat is a lovely, intelligent, honest woman who's loved her brother, honored her parents and was raised in the school of hard knocks. I asked her to look at and comment on the black and white photo of Larry in his catcher's outfit when he was a boy. She smiled and said, "That's my brother! He's probably thinking: When the ball comes, I've got to get this ball! When that ball comes, I'm ready! We all needed a person like Larry, he's always had such a good demeanor and always a happy-go-lucky guy. We don't get to see each other as often as we'd like because we don't drive any longer."

Pat is such a handsome, poised, wonderful woman, mother and grandmother and a recent widow. In her senior years, she maintains her family photos and sits at her computer working on the family's genealogy. She said, "I enjoy it very much and it keeps me busy!"

As most of us in our youth, we learned to play catch with our dad. If you're one of the kids growing up in the inner-city, you may not have a chance, if ever, to play catch and start out as Larry did. But if you're one of these kids reading this, take a page out of Larry's story—you could be the next Willie Mays.

A wonderful quote by Thomas Paine captures this story very succinctly. He wrote:

> "I love the man that can smile in trouble, that can gather strength from distress, and grow brave by reflection. 'Tis the business of little minds to shrink, but he whose heart is firm, and whose conscience approves his conduct, will pursue his principals until death."

As we all move on through time, we find a spacious sense of the amplitude of life's possibilities and eager hopefulness within our human spirit.

Life has taught me that it has better plans, so I try every day to submerge my desires and dreams in a pensive willingness and accept what the future brings, then patiently wait again. I believe there's a pattern in our lives that's already pre-destined and more splendid than our short-sighted view can formulate.

In closing, it's important to listen to someone's story with an understanding and an open mind. If you're a good listener, you're half-way there to enlightenment, possible secrets or even surprises.

A beautiful quote from dearly departed, Maya, sums up our historical American era:

> "History, despite it's heart-wrenching pain, cannot be unlived, but if faced with courage, need not be lived again."
>
> —Maya Angelou

★ ★ ★

Addendum

We were all elated to find out that in September of this year (2015), Larry had finally received " a substantial l ump sum like most of the other players had gotten and is now awarded his monthly MLB pension." I was compelled to add this Addendum to the book to reflect this tremendous news. Thanks M LB for s tepping up t o the p late for Larry. A s we took on the challenge of assisting Larry to obtain his major league baseball pension, since he was denied at the time of the initial interviews with him, we felt we could make an impact.

Based on my research background and volunteered to do so, I had kept Larry LeGrande updated every step of the way of the writing and research process. Being a career-driven market researcher for over 20 years, I found myself digging deeper into the root cause of why Larry was not awarded his pension. He attempted several times to submit what little evidence he possessed of his baseball tenure, but to no avail—the doors were closed in his face for decades. Over the span of several years, I had contacted numerous libraries in the country, sifted through newspapers, made numerous phone calls, spoke to other Negro League players, joined online groups and read several historical books.

My obsession to right this wrong compelled me to intermittently pause my working career for these years dedicated to Larry LeGrande. In July of 2014, I wrote to various attorneys, MLB, ESPN and BAT and provided them with faxes and evidence (at their request) that Larry LeGrande, did, in fact play all four years in the Negro Leagues. No individuals every returned my calls, faxes nor emails on this issue. However, they had the evidence of my efforts, in-hand and they worked the issues behind the scenes unbeknown to me with a successful result for Larry LeGrande.

Although our income suffered during this time, the ultimate goal to research, document and publish the evidence in this book was exceptionally overwhelming. These activities in this writing project resulted in extremely labor-intensive and time-consuming efforts.

My ultimate goal was to correct and publish a historical oversight that caused a man deep and painful grief for over a half a century. Moreover, in order to correct this disparity and establish the proof to the powers-that-be that Larry, did in fact, meet the requirements for his baseball pension.

As one attempts or commits to a project of this magnitude of writing someone's life story, there are hurdles and challenges that appear.

Life's complications got in the way and caused unfortunate delays in the writing of this story, but perseverance, focus and the burning desire to tell Larry's story remained in the forefront of our lives during this time.

The story was finally and successfully published, but not without frustrations and difficulties.

As soon as the manuscript was complete, the next challenge was finding and submitting the work to over a couple dozen publishers. Out of these couple dozen publishers, two responded with extreme interest in this biography, all of which took months of preparation and communications. One of the two aforementioned publishers happened to be one of the largest publishing houses from New York City! Wow!!! That meant national distribution, potential advertising, marketing dollars and a fast-track to publicize Larry's story. It was exceptionally exciting and overwhelming. This New York publisher explained that they would be happy to accept my manuscript, but we were small fish and there were many more bigger fish in the queue. So the start date to publish the book would be in three and half years.

After this disappointment, it was decision time, since the only other publisher that came knocking at our door was Tate Publishing. Their approach meant that we would shoulder the burden of publishing, printing, marketing and advertising costs.

But whatever circumstances, giving up on telling Larry's story when and wherever possible--pushing every avenue of promoting this piece of history--was not an option. The costs and expenses of this challenge at times had been overwhelming, but individuals' response in the public eye has been more than receptive-it's been embraced and welcomed. This financial burden of publishing is ugly, yes, but necessary in order to keep the promise to Larry.

There were great plans to make this publication a success, but just after contracting with the publisher, we were informed by another publisher that these types of publications do not sell well and that meant never recouping our personal expenses and publishing costs. Still we plow forward. Why?

. Simply the right thing to do!! In never asking Larry to cover any expenses, travel or otherwise to complete the task and at no labor charge to write his biography as a biographer normally would, it remains a matter of importance to capture this glimpse of history of a young boy who became a key baseball player and best friend to Satchel Paige.

Getting back to the decision, waiting more than three years risked the fact that Larry would no longer be with us as well as facing immediate out-of-pocket expenses with no national distribution and no advertising/ marketing dollars with all financial efforts directly on us – the decision was an easy one --- get the story out ASAP!

In the final thought process, getting Larry's story out to commence his closure and attempt to begin his healing process with resolution, played heavily and was indeed, a priority. No amount of cost, time effort, marketing or otherwise was worth delaying the story three and a half years to have a better outcome and to give Larry a voice. It's vitally important that this snapshot in time is shared with the public as well as for generations to come— who hopefully do not have to re-live this dark time in America's history.

✷ ✷ ✷

Research Acknowledgments

M any *Thanks* to the historians in the libraries who helped make this writing possible in the United States and in Canada namely:

Birmingham Alabama Public Library
Center for Negro League Baseball Research
Columbus Ohio Library
Inside Pitch Promotions
Kansas City Missouri Public Library
Library of Congress, Humanities
and Social Sciences Division
Memphis Tennessee and Shelby County
Room, Memphis Public Library
National Baseball Hall of Fame,
Giamatti Research Center
Nova Scotia Sport Hall of Fame Museum

Ohio Historical Society
Public Broadcasting of Atlanta Georgia
St. Petersburg Museum of History
University of Memphis Tennessee Libraries

Individuals within these organizations who helped to make this writing a success and to bring forward this important piece of history for all to read. History is something we that can all reach out and touch, and sometimes, feel, smell and even hear. Whether it be through documents, photos, memories, museums, food or music our historians should be commended for their part in upholding our American History. For this, I'm grateful.

Many thanks go to the Tate Publishing house, and all the individuals who labored over this book to help me get this story to you. Their mission is faith-based as mine is to impart this labor of inspiration in the hopes that the reader will be enlightened and find hopefulness in moments of darkness.

★ ★ ★

Bibliography

1. *The Roanoke Times*, "Baseball Has Changed," March 30, 2006, Page 1, Front Page.
2. *The Roanoke Times*, "LeGrande: Bitter Memories Gnawed at Him," March 30, 2006, (Continued from Page 1), Page 5.
3. *Press & Sun-Bulletin*, "LeGrande's Baseball Days Bittersweet," September 18, 2003, Section D.
4. *The Roanoke Times, Extra*, "Jackie Robinson Blazed the Train...And Others, Like Larry LeGrande of Roanoke, Fought to Finish the Journey," April 6, 1997, Page 1, Front Page; *Extra*, Page 5.
5. *Winston-Salem Journal*, "Separate Diamonds," State, November 23, 2003, Page 1, Front Page, Page B5.
6. *The Roanoke Times*, "LeGrande Loves Baseball Again," December 12, 2002, Sports Edition, Front Page, Section C; Page C2.

7. *Virginia General Assembly*, Website. 2006. Agreed to by the House of Delegates, January 13, 2006. Agreed to by the Senate, January 19, 2006.

8. *News and Observer*, "Former Player Goes to Bat for the Negro Leagues," May 21, 2007.

9. *The Roanoke Times*, "Baseball Deals Some Cruel Blows," May 27, 1960. Sports of the Times. The Billboard.

10. *The St. Petersburg Times*, "Yanks End Lang Season with Win Over Tribe" December 11, 1959, Page 2-C.

11. *Satchel Paige and Company, Essays on the Kansas City Monarchs their Greatest Star and the Negro Leagues.* Published 2007. Leslie A. Heaphy.

12. *Anderson Herald*, "Falstaffs Clash With Memphis 9," August 6, 1957, Page 7. Anderson Indiana.

13. *The Ohio Sentinel*, "Clowns, Barons Tangle in Stadium Sunday p.m.", July 12, 1958, Page 31.

14. *The Chicago Defender*, "West Defeats East, 8–7 in 11th", August 22, 1959, Page 24.

15. *Lima News*, "Monarchs Muscles Magnificent, Bombs Away! Kansas City Homers Ruin Metros, *7–1*". Lima, Ohio 1959.

16. *The Morning Herald*, Hagerstown, Maryland. July 16, 1959. "Tonight at 8, Negro Teams to Clash at Stadium." The Morning Herald.

17. *New York Age*, "Detroit Clowns with 'Goose and Sweetwater' Face Kansas City Monarchs in Stadium Sunday". Page 39. August 16, 1958.

18. *The New York Times*, "Monarchs, Clowns Divide at Stadium", Page 24. August 18, 1958.

19. *The Osh Kosh Daily Northwestern*, "Immortal Satchel to Appear Saturday", Page 15. June 14, 1963.

20. *The Osh Kosh Daily Northwestern*, "Satchel Paige All-Stars Take Late Inning Victory", Page 15. June 17, 1963.

21. *The Hays Daily News*, "Large Crowd Expected for Benefit Game Thursday Evening", Page 11. July 25, 1962.

22. *The News Palladium*, "Twins' Airs Costly As Monarchs Win, 4–2," Section 2, Page 3. August 7, 1964.

23. *The Iola Register*, "Paige's Team Loses in the Ninth", Page 6. August 1, 1961.

24. *The Muscatine Journal and News Tribune*, "Sox Split with Nats, Monarchs," Page 8, June 21, 1961.

25. *The Wellsville Daily Reporter*, Page 7. August 16, 1961.

26. The St. Petersburg Independent, "Sixth Run Ninth Whips Saints", Page 10-A. April 15, 1960.

27. *The Roanoke Times*, "Daughter Refuses to Sign Papers to Close Sale for Mother. Family at Odds Over Sale of Old Home." Front Page, Page A2. September 22, 2000.

28. *The Roanoke Times*, "Home Depot Revives Plan for 220 Site". May 17, 2005.

29. *Associated Press*, Charitable Fund to Pay Pensions". May 17, 2004.

30. *Joe Henry's Letter* to BAT and MLB, September 13, 2004.

31. *BAT Letter* from James Martin, April 11, 2008.

32. *The Bleacher Report*, MLB Isn't Paying Pensions to Herb Washington and Other Persons of Color, Doug Gladstone, July 17, 2012.

33. Public Broadcasting Atlanta, Video interviews with former Negro League Players, *"Safe At Home Plate"*. 1993.

34. *The Post-Standard,* "Clowns Defeat Trotters (s.b. Monarchs) at MacArthur Stadium." August 29, 1958.

35. "Clowns-Monarchs at Stadium." August 16, 1958. (No Citation. Article Not Scanned. ANS.)

36. *The New York Times*, "East's Negro Nine Defeats West, 6–5", September 1, 1958.

37. *St. Petersburg Times*, "Saints Fire Charnofsky; Successor Due Today", "The Untouchables", by Bill Beck, Page 17. July 18, 1960.

38. *The Sunday Independent*, (St. Petersburg), "Saints Clicking Just in Time", May 8, 1960.

39. *The St. Petersburg Times*, "Anglanda Whips Orlando 3 To 1", May 7, 1960.

40. *The Kansas City Star*, "Women and Minorities", April 25, 1999.

41. *St. Petersburg Times*, "The Front Office." Bill Beck, June 1960.

42. Powell, Larry, *Black Barons of Birmingham: The South's Greatest Negro League Team and its Players*, June 13, 2009.

Research & References

Aristotle, Greek philosopher. (384–322 BC), "The Art of Rhetoric", sect. 6, ch. 2.4.

Center for Negro League Baseball Research. Website.

"I Will Never Forget", Interviews with 39 Former Negro League Players. Brent Kelley.

Interview with Larry LeGrande's sister, "Pat" Ruth Davis. July 25, 2014.

Interview with James Ayers, Canadian Baseball Player. October 6, 2014.

James A. Riley, *The Biographical Encyclopedia of the Negro Baseball Leagues, New York: Carroll & Graf Publishers, Inc., 1994.*

Ken Burns, *Film Documentary, "Baseball".*

National Register of Historic Places, *"Historic Resources of the 18th and Vine area of Kansas City, Missouri."* January, 1987.

NLBM Legacy 2000 Players' Reunion Alumni Book, Kansas City Missouri: Negro Leagues Baseball Museum, Inc., 2000.

Oliver L. Brown et. al. v. the Board of Education of Topeka, Kansas. National Archives.

The Medical District, Memphis Heritage, Inc. for the Memphis Landmarks Commission, April 2003.

About the Author

My earlier career comprised of working as a Market and Competitive Intelligence Manager and Director within marketing organizations of small to large high-tech companies and various vertical industries. I've been an entrepreneur and have owned and operated several businesses. My having children just wasn't in the cards. Thus, research, writing, reporting for key executives and leadership teams to assist in their strategic decision-making became my passion. During my latter 16 years with 8—layoffs, buyouts and downsizings, I took up web design to diversify my career and extend the artist within.

I previously lived with my family in Massachusetts and Southern New Hampshire. A software development company relocated me in 1999, where I've remained in the beautiful state of North Carolina and married in 2003.

My educations consists of an Associates in Business from Castle College in New Hampshire; Bachelors in Marketing from Rivier College in New Hampshire; and Master's in Management from Lesley University in Cambridge, Massachusetts.

Canadian-born, I retained my native tongue and have been a United States citizen for over 40 years. Growing up I'd frequently hear the stories my dad would tell me about the Negro Ballplayers. My father, born and raised in Canada, truly loved playing with the Negro Leagues when they traveled and barnstormed their way through Canada's countryside. Many of the Negro Leagues and Canadian teams sat and talked in diners or just sat in the fields where they played. There was no segregation there, nor racial hatred and tensions—just good, competitive games.

I want to share Larry's biography with the world, as his story stirred my soul, I hope it will do so for the reader. Larry's story really touched me the day I met him as I progressed through the interviews, what emerged was a stream of emotions, injustices, disappointments, shocking events and laughter. It's proven to be a very interesting, enlightening and educational accumulation of knowledge and I'm grateful to Larry for having shared his life with me.